PRAISE FOR *CHARACTER IS DESTINY*

"A fascinating window into the life and work of Swedish businessman and European Round Table of Industrialists founder Pehr Gyllenhammar. Whether recounting his childhood during World War II, his years as Volvo's CEO, or his little known work as a Track Two diplomat in the Middle East, Gyllenhammar is always engaging and intelligent, offering an unflinching assessment of international business, US and European politics, and democracies under siege. Like its author, with whom I share a decades-old friendship, *Character is Destiny* is by turns insightful, amusing, and refreshingly direct."

—Henry Kissinger

"Business leader, diplomat, humanist and global citizen—Pehr Gyllenhammar has led a life of fruitful endeavor marked by the highest standards of integrity. This distinguished Swede has cleverly decided to write his impressive autobiography in English. *Character is Destiny* should be read by all aspiring leaders who want to build bridges, not walls."

—David Rockefeller, Jr.

"Pehr Gyllenhammar is one of the most respected and thoughtful leaders of his generation. His long awaited second book promises to be an important contribution to thinking about how to make the world a safer and better place through the lens of business and diplomacy."

—Glenn D. Lowry

"A sentient being of remarkable purpose in the pursuit of human qualities. Pehr's passion, curiosity, humility and absolute integrity have inspired countless individuals. The range of his perception belies his experience. I look inward after our dialogues. Pehr's legacy deserves this personal narrative for generations to ponder."

—David Thomson

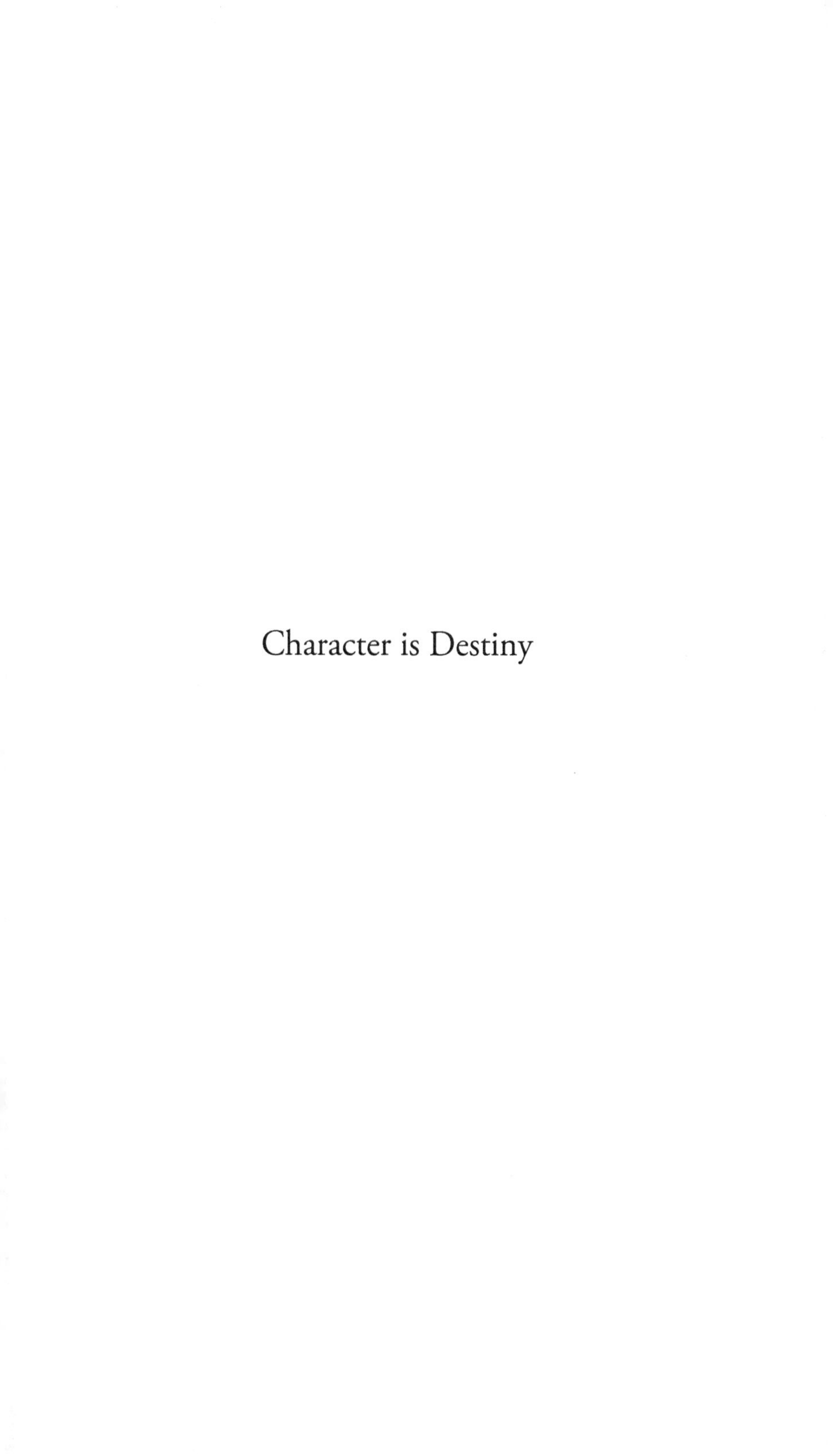

Character is Destiny

CHARACTER IS DESTINY

Reflections on
INNOVATION & INTEGRITY
from
VOLVO'S LONGEST SERVING CEO

PEHR GYLLENHAMMAR

NEW YORK
LONDON • NASHVILLE • MELBOURNE • VANCOUVER

CHARACTER IS DESTINY

Reflections on Innovation & Integrity from Volvo's Longest Serving CEO

Published in New York, New York, by Morgan James Publishing. Morgan James is a trademark of Morgan James, LLC. www.MorganJamesPublishing.com

ISBN 9781642799743 paperback
ISBN 9781642799736 case laminate
ISBN 9781642799750 eBook
Library of Congress Control Number: 2019958029

Cover and Interior Design by:
Chris Treccani
www.3dogcreative.net

Cover Photo by:
Filip Erlind

To my wife Lee, my brilliant partner and inspiration,
and to our extraordinary daughter Barrett,
the rising sun of our lives.

TABLE OF CONTENTS

FOREWORD

For nine years, Pehr G Gyllenhammar was voted "Sweden´s most admired man." This is reason enough to be interested in Gyllenhammar the man, and to learn more about him. We all know it is windy atop the high hills of accomplishment. How has it been possible for him not just to become so successful, but to maintain his good reputation for so long? In this book, Gyllenhammar tells you in his own words what it took to rise to the top, and what it takes, in his opinion, to stay there.

It was a very young Gyllenhammar who was appointed CEO of Volvo, a position he kept for 24 years. Volvo began in Sweden, but during Gyllenhammar's tenure it became more and more global in its activities. Swedes were proud to see Volvo cars wherever they went, all over the world.

It is no surprise that the shareholders and car-owners were satisfied with Volvo's dynamic leader. What I find quite interesting, however, is that he inspired such sympathy and support in the labor unions. Step by step, Gyllenhammar worked to build a very special relationship with Volvo's workers. He created a corporate structure in which the workers enjoyed more dialogue and participation, and as a result, wasted less energy fighting. The unions knew that their company had a strong leader who was also good listener. This created trust in Gyllenhammar not just as a CEO, but as a person.

Volvo remained Pehr Gyllenhammar´s first priority throughout his time there. But very early on he also became involved with matters concerning European infrastructure. As Europe's countries, through political and economic cooperation, were growing stronger and more united, Gyllenhammar saw new possibilities for everyone. His vision was that industry and its leaders should play an active role in developing Europe through new large-scale infrastructural projects.

In 1983 Gyllenhammar took the initiative in founding the European Round Table of Industrialists. The idea behind this organization was that European enterprises should strengthen their competitiveness and find new projects that would stimulate development and cooperation throughout Europe. To enable faster and easier movement of people and goods, new tunnels, bridges and high-speed trains were needed. Gyllenhammar described these as "missing links" in Europe.

One of these missing links was a bridge for cars and trains across Öresund between Sweden and Denmark. This issue had been discussed for decades, but without result. At the end of the 1980s, Sweden and Denmark finally reached an agreement to build the bridge. At that time I was Prime Minister in Sweden, and I can confirm that the work done by Mr Gyllenhammar and the European Round Table of Industrialists was very helpful in promoting the project.

In 1984, Gyllenhammar was asked to join the board of Reuters Holdings PLC. His participation demonstrates not just his broad capacity, but also how well-known and well-respected he had become around the world. The doors to Presidents, Prime Ministers and Ministers for Foreign Affairs were all open to him. He had friendly relations with Singapore President Lee Kuan Yew, with King Hussein of Jordan, and with David Rockefeller, to name just a few.

Pehr G Gyllenhammar is a true democrat and a person of firm liberal values. As CEO of Volvo he dissociated himself early on from the apartheid policy of South Africa. Today, he is deeply troubled that extreme right wing, nationalistic, populist and fascist forces are gaining ground in the world. He is very outspoken about the dangers we are facing, and has made his position very clear: Democracy is in danger!

In this book you will meet a colorful and charismatic person, a man with whom I have been friends for many years. Through the experiences Gyllenhammar recounts, you will encounter his unique perspective on industry, modern history, and politics. Gyllenhammar makes no secret here of the one quality he values above all others, the one quality that any person, corporation or community must possess in order to achieve the kind of long-term success that Gyllenhammar himself has enjoyed: integrity.

Ingvar Carlsson
Former Prime Minister of Sweden

INTRODUCTION

Communication

Communicate: *from the classical Latin commūnicāt-...to take a share in, to make a sharer (in), to share out, to associate, to impart, to discuss together, to consult together, to bring into common use, make generally accessible.*

—Oxford English Dictionary

It has been fifty years since I published my first book, *Towards the Turn of the Century, at Random*, a work that addressed my fundamental concern with the ability of democracy to safeguard and manage our collective future. Five decades of that envisioned "future" are now behind me, and over their course I have worked with people from all walks of life, in endeavors that include those of industry, diplomacy, politics, and the arts. In my experience, with each passing decade of increasing global interdependence there has been a growing, critical scarcity of the value-driven individual and institution.

In a world already undergoing dramatic political changes, we are, as I write this, experiencing a profound disruption to daily life in the wake of the coronavirus—one of the deadliest global pandemics in modern history. Coronavirus has upended almost every aspect of life, leaving vast numbers of people unemployed, disrupting important international exchanges of goods and services, gutting the stock market and economy, and leaving entire nations reeling in confusion and shock as they struggle to come to terms with the loss of life and instability now pervading the world. There is no way to know how long the pandemic will continue, what the ultimate toll will be, or whether and when a vaccine will be developed. What we do know is that the world will not be the same in the aftermath of this extraordinary calamity. Throughout this crisis, the American political arena has demonstrated an appalling deficiency of leadership.

The elected president of the US is self-obsessed, dangerously impulsive, poorly educated, and alarmingly uninformed. Because the democratic system creates a tabula rasa for each newly-elected commander in chief, he has been able to largely eradicate many of the people, policies, and platforms of the previous administration, often dismantling old structures but failing to replace them. Democracy's predilection for short-termism has never been more damaging than in Washington today, where the prevailing Republican Party has virtually closed ranks behind the president even as allegations of serious political, business, and personal misconduct increase, and a constitutional crisis seems all but inevitable.

What has made it possible for one man to instigate the collapse of a 250-year-old political democracy? One considerable factor is the prevailing climate of dishonesty and double-talk legitimized and championed by President Donald Trump, a man who literally lies with impunity, both off the record and on, often compounding previous lies with new ones.

While America has presented the world with the most blatant (and therefore the most dangerous) scenarios of rapid-fire political and cultural disintegration, similar problems have arisen in numerous other parts of the world as well. Nationalist movements in Europe are on the rise as is terrorism, and Brexit has given a clear indication of the extent of the European Union's instability. The breakdown of our ability to communicate cogently coupled with our increasing tolerance for—or unwillingness to censure—double-talk, hypocrisy, and outright prevarication in our leaders has put the whole world at risk.

The decline in our ability to communicate honestly and with integrity is a dangerous signpost. All cultures are to some extent predicated on shared identity and experience, and communal and historical connection. Language is the bastion of all of these. A leader with the power to control language and communication is one who will be able to maintain broad political and social power, for better or worse. In contemporary society, we depend upon the media and upon a free press as the most reliable means for the communication of news and information. A political leader who openly wages war on the media poses a serious risk to culture and society, one that cannot be ignored.

And who is doing the listening—who comprises most of the collective body of people that enable a leader to take and keep power? They are largely the regular workingmen and women of the society or institution in question. They are the people with whom I've had some of the most rewarding and gratifying experiences of my professional life. On the factory floor at Volvo and beyond, I've found the labor force to be more open-minded, honest, and fair than any other group, and I've long admired their ability to see things that even their white-collar counterparts could not.

The mutually respectful relationship I've had with working people over the years is not a result of my being a highly skilled speaker—since I don't believe that I am—it has come rather because our interactions were always unvarnished, honest, and direct. This is the source of my long-standing conviction that when one strives to narrow the gap between what one thinks and how one acts, the resulting correlation engenders trust and followership—not by capitulation, but through the consensus that comes from interacting with people on equal terms as adults with agency, and by addressing their higher-order psychological needs.

And so, a good half century after writing *Towards the Turn of the Century, at Random*, as a young man of thirty-four, I return to this somewhat familiar but shifting territory. With the benefit and hindsight of decades of good fortune, I've been privileged to come to know a number of great institutions and remarkable people. Some are familiar names, while others remain unsung heroes who accomplished great things in relative anonymity. In reflecting on what qualities these leaders of many different kinds might share, there is one compelling commonality: profound integrity. Every person or organization that I have experienced as highly effectual is one who held its actions and communications to the highest ethical standard, with unflinching alignment between words and deeds, regardless of how such forthrightness would be received by the prevailing establishment. And each of these individuals has had the intuitive understanding that a true leader of any capacity must possess and demonstrate an authentic intolerance for injustice.

In sharing some of my experiences over the years with individuals and groups that have had exceptional impact on the world, I hope to demonstrate by their example the power of integrity in speech and action, and how the two act as a singular power through the art of communication. At a time when people around the world are anxious and pessimistic about the future, and democracies and institutions we have seen as unassailable are threatening to crumble, it is imperative that we strive to communicate in a way that reflects a principled stance and commitment to what is upright, and that we demand that quality in our leaders. From an individual standpoint, a long-term view of the world is predicated on having the method and means to begin the architecture of a sustainable future. I believe that neither the method nor the means have changed in the last fifty years; they remain rooted in a system of ethics and values that adhere to an unyielding core of integrity. As such, sustainable approaches—whether to business, national policy, or to the way we choose to live or consume—require that we proceed simply, with economy and directness of intent, committed to prioritizing what is important and what is right not just for ourselves, but for everyone.

Toronto
April 2020

CHAPTER ONE

Truth

Truth: *from Old English triewe (West Saxon), treowe (Mercian) "faithful, trustworthy, honest, steady in adhering to promises, friends, etc.," from Proto-Germanic *treuwaz "having or characterized by good faith" (source also of Old Frisian triuwi, Dutch getrouw, Old High German gatriuwu, German treu, Old Norse tryggr, Danish tryg, Gothic triggws "faithful, trusty"), from PIE *drew-o-, a suffixed form of the root *deru- "be firm, solid, steadfast."*

–Oxford English Dictionary

My relationship with the Reuters Group dates back to 1984, the year it was floated as a public company in London, when I was first asked to join the board of directors of Reuters Holdings, PLC. My long-standing affinity for commitment to integrity made Reuters—with its mandate to adhere to the Trust Principles of ethics established in 1941—a very appealing institution. In advance of the flotation, it was decided that three non-press directors should be added to the board—one American, one British, and one European (since, as we have now been informed, Britain is not part of Europe). The board approved the addition of US Citicorp chairman Walter Wriston, UK chairman of Courtaulds Christopher Hogg, and me (then CEO of Volvo) representing the rest of Europe. A new entity—named the Reuters Founders Share Company Ltd.—was formed, and the new corporate charter specified that the board of directors be charged with overseeing that the company continue to adhere to the original Trust Principles, specifically:

1. That Thomson Reuters shall at no time pass into the hands of any one interest, group, or faction;
2. That the integrity, independence, and freedom from bias of Thomson Reuters shall at all times be fully preserved;
3. That Thomson Reuters shall supply unbiased and reliable news services to newspapers, news agencies, broadcasters, and other media subscribers and to businesses, governments, institutions, individuals, and others with whom Thomson Reuters has or may have contracts;
4. That Thomson Reuters shall pay due regard to the many interests which it serves in addition to those of the media; and
5. That no effort shall be spared to expand, develop, and adapt the news and other services and products so as to maintain its leading position in the international news and information business.

At that time in the 1980s, Reuters had enjoyed a reputation as one of the world's leading news agencies for over a century. Renowned as much for its commitment to incorporating the newest technologies as for its integrity, Reuters' beginnings were characterized by ingenious strategies devised to work around shortcomings and inconsistencies in the existing communications network.

On October 17, 1851, engineers of the Submarine Telegraph Company successfully completed laying the first functional submarine communications cable across the English Channel. That same evening, the first electronic message between England and France was transmitted and received. It was an accomplishment significant enough to merit the immediate conveyance of the message to the Queen and to the Duke of Wellington.

Shortly thereafter, Paul Julius Reuter arrived in London to open a transmission service to convey stock quotes to and from Paris using the new Calais-Dover cable. His focus on finding ways to allow for the rapid communication of accurate information was already well established. News agencies were regularly sending stories via overland telegraph cables in Europe, but in 1850 the line of connections from one side of the continent to the other still contained gaps. Reuter came up with the idea of bridging the telegraph gap between Brussels and Aachen by using carrier pigeons. Up until this time, the most reliable prevailing method of bridging the gap was to send messages by train, an eight-hour journey. Reuter's birds could make the same seventy-six-mile journey in an impressive two hours. His pigeon post remained the fastest method of disseminating the news until the Belgium-Germany telegraph gap was closed in April of 1851. Mindful of ongoing plans to establish a telegraph connection between England and France, Reuter relocated to London, financial capital of the world.

Over the course of several decades, the name Reuter became synonymous with rapid news circulation, in large part due to Paul Julius Reuter's continued focus on finding ways to speed the dissemination of news after its arrival from the United States, a country that would not have a lasting cable connection with Europe until 1856. News traveled eastward from America's east coast across the Atlantic via steamer, taking an average of about nine days to reach Europe. Reuter hired men to work as lookouts posted near Crookhaven Harbor on Ireland's southwestern coast. These lookouts scanned the horizon for the approach of mail-carrying steamships. By arrangement, whatever steamship happened to be carrying mail from Reuter's US news agent, Associated Press, would turn on a blue signal light when they neared the Irish coast. As soon as a blue-lit steamer came within view of one of the lookouts, the crew on Reuter's own tender Marseilles would be alerted to intercept the inbound steamship. Also by previous arrangement, the purser on the incoming steamer would pack all mail addressed to Reuter in watertight canisters, which were tossed overboard to be retrieved with nets by the Marseilles crew.

Getting hold of incoming US news before anyone else provided no advantage unless it could also be circulated to and across Europe. Reuter had a system for that, too. He purchased a private cable connection between Crookhaven and Cork, some seventy miles to the northeast. Time-sensitive news retrieved by the Marseilles from the floating containers was telegraphed from Crookhaven, and from Cork it was retransmitted to London. In this way, breaking news from Reuter arrived in the London telegraph a minimum of several hours before the same mail steamer that carried it across the Atlantic could reach Liverpool. These details are telling in giving an idea of the lengths and expense Paul Julius Reuter was willing to go to in order to ensure he had the earliest possible access to transatlantic news and be the first European source of developing news stories. This was far more than merely a nominal accomplishment, as evidenced by Reuters breaking the news story of the assassination of Abraham Lincoln, an event that in addition to its social and political import had a direct effect on the financial market.

Over the next several decades, Reuters expanded across European countries, and ultimately across continents, following the growing telegraph-accessible locations to the Far East and South America. In 1923, the agency became the first to send stock quotes via radio, transmitting them from London to Europe in Morse code. Reuters remained consistent in placing a priority on incorporating the newest technologies into their communications network, adopting the teleprinter to distribute stories to newspapers throughout London, and reinventing their own position in the market with the introduction of the computerized Reuters Stockmaster real-time price retrieval system in 1964. In 1973, President Nixon dismantled the Bretton Woods Agreement, which had obliged member nations to establish a fixed rate of external exchange by linking the rate to the gold standard. Reuters anticipated the widespread effects of the "Nixon shock" by creating and launching the Reuter Monitor Money Rates Services—an international foreign exchange network. The Reuter Monitor enabled contributing institutions to input their exchange rates and allowed subscribers to retrieve and view on video display terminals all of the participating banks' exchange rates for each currency—information that had never before been accessible from a single source.

I was pleased and optimistic about joining the Reuters board, and remained longer than almost anyone else. When I felt it was time for me to move on, I gave my notice. I did not expect the response I received. "Pehr," I was told, "you cannot leave the family. We would like to propose instead that you become a board member of our Founders Share Company." I found that I did see Reuters as a family of sorts, and so I accepted that proposal, and several months later was asked to become chairman of the Founders Share Company board.

During the course of my three five-year terms on the FSC board, my high esteem for the company never faltered. It marked a significant part of my life, as I took very seriously the task of overseeing the company and ensuring that the Trust Principles were upheld and respected in the company's conduct. In their essence, the principles are independence, integrity, and freedom from bias. Both the principles themselves and the importance of safeguarding them truly spoke to me. The model Reuters established appealed to my belief in the great importance of both ethical standards in the corporate world, and in the need to protect the free press, regardless of what that entailed. At times this even necessitated intervening in the actions of another director. When board member Rupert Murdoch went over the 15 percent ownership threshold for outside shareholders, for example, it was my responsibility to step in and directly challenge Murdoch's actions. I will admit that after telling him it was unacceptable to pass the threshold and informing him that he must sell down, I held my breath to see if he would simply tell me to go to hell. But after several days, he did sell down, reducing his company shares to the appropriate and authorized amount.

After the end of my third five-year term (and having passed the three-term time limit) I was happy to accept the position of chairman of the board of the Founders Share Company and continue into the next decade with Reuters. I wanted to do everything in my power to keep the company on its course. It was a powerful and occasionally humbling experience to observe the many ways—great and small—in which the Reuters people evaluated and sometimes adjusted their own actions to ensure that they were in keeping with the Trust Principles.

On the evening of September 11, 2001, as a shaken world absorbed the news of the devastating terror attacks in the United

States, David Wenig, Reuters president of Investment Banking and Brokerage Services, requested that the large electronic billboards outside of Reuters' London office display an image of the American flag, to communicate England's solidarity with America. Feedback came in from a number of editorial managers asking that the flag be removed, as it could be construed to be an indication of bias. I happened to be in New York on that day, visiting the Lazard financial management firm in my capacity as their senior advisor and managing director.

I had arrived at Lazard's Rockefeller Center office quite early in the morning, and a colleague and a secretary were the only other people in the sixty-second-floor office. It was an absolutely beautiful day, cool and clear, the skyline of the city crisp and vivid against the bright blue sky. On one of the television monitors, I heard the breaking news that a plane had just hit a Manhattan skyscraper. The southern-facing exposure of the Lazard offices provides a bird's-eye view of Manhattan from the East River to the Hudson. After hearing the news, my colleague and I went to the window from which we could clearly see a vast plume of brown smoke pouring from the north tower of the World Trade Center. At that moment, we saw a second plane approaching rapidly from the southwest. We stood shoulder to shoulder watching with disbelief as the plane hit the south tower, sending a massive fireball shooting into the sky. I don't believe either of us spoke—what was there to say? The sight was so dramatic—so viscerally brutal—it is virtually impossible to convey to anyone who did not see it with their own eyes.

After the towers collapsed, the scene in lower Manhattan was one of utter devastation, and the scale of human suffering unbearable. I was not only deeply shaken by what I had seen, I was not at all sure that more attacks were not on the way. I had no intention of getting into the elevator to descend sixty-two floors, so I remained where I was. My colleague followed suit. At about 11 a.m., I heard voices and saw several policemen entering the office. They seemed surprised to see us, as the building had been closed off and no one was supposed to be inside. My colleague and I took the sixy-two-floor elevator ride in silence, emerging in the plaza with no idea where to go or what to do. Like countless others, I was marooned, unable to travel out of the city. I followed the events surrounding the London Reuters' office and the American flag by telephone from my hotel. I was both touched by their impulse to display solidarity and impressed with their difficult decision to take the flag down. To me, it represented the pinnacle of integrity, and embodied everything I admired about the organization.

In an internal newsletter dated September 19, 2001, Wenig discussed the painful decision to comply and remove the flag, saying, "It was and is clear on reflection that the ideals of independence and objectivity go to the heart of what we are as a company. These pillars cannot be selectively retracted when we feel passion, or when we believe that right and wrong are so plainly clear. In fact, the trust principles are reinforced most powerfully when they are stretched and challenged the furthest."

This was a remarkable demonstration of what it takes to protect ethical principles in a corporate world. The Trust doesn't pose a burden of expense or bureaucracy on the corporation, but it does preclude prioritizing profits over everything else. The fact of Reuters' longevity as a company is evidence that with a long-term view, the Trust Principles have served the institution extremely well. It is also a clear indication of the clarity of vision and flexibility of mind of the Trust founders, not dissimilar to that of the authors of the US Constitution—anticipating in the extreme long term the needs and obstacles of the company—creating a structure of preservation that is neither too specific nor too broad, but that will safeguard the principles without compromising the company's ability to operate, expand, and adapt to the times.

For all its core ethos and latitude, the Trust is by no means immutable—human vigilance and foresight remain crucial to its safekeeping. In Michael Nelson's memoir *Castro and Stockmaster: A Life in Reuters*, the company's former general manager writes, "The Founders Share became vulnerable every time the protracted agenda over an EU Takeover Directive fired up again. The call for 'one share one vote,' if carried, could have wiped it out. We pressed the case that the Founders Share should be viewed as a qualitative rather than economic instrument, designed to protect Reuters core values, but having no economic value of its own. In this way, we sought to distinguish it from the majority of 'golden shares' designed to uphold the interests of a particular person, family, or other grouping."

I can only hope that the unbroken line of individuals that have carried the torch of the principles forward year after year will continue indefinitely. What is at stake is more than just a corporate ethos and goes beyond even the imperative of preserving the value of media organizations. Lack of integrity—and a media that does not stick to good journalistic practice—can create a very dangerous situation for the rest of the world. America felt the full extent of journalism's power when Katharine Graham and two of her Washington Post reporters had the courage and tenacity to investigate the Watergate break-in to its culmination—resulting in the downfall of the president himself. But over forty years later, the country is reeling from the one-two punch of an assault on the free press and the prevalence of television "news" shows that are thinly disguised propaganda machines. For every just force, there is an opposing unjust force, and the power to vanquish a corrupt president can manifest as the power to protect one.

The present struggle over the freedom of the press and the maintenance of truth in reporting and disseminating the news can be traced back at least as far as the period between the World Wars in the twentieth century, when governments threatened to take control of information. In 1941, Reuters took strong measures to prevent being taken over (specifically by the British government); it was then that the Reuters Trust was formed and Trust Principles put in place. In the 1980s another kind of crisis arose: the danger that information might be taken over by the superwealthy. If there is cynicism in the belief that anything and anyone can be bought, it is only because it happens with increasing frequency.

At the heart of these issues is the preservation of truth—of conscience itself—by maintaining the independence of the means of producing and disseminating information. A September 2017 Reuters US poll found that national confidence in the American press had risen to 48 percent, up from 39 percent the previous year. That is grounds for cautious optimism, but it is still only one small step back from the brink. Trust is crucial, but there must also be the means for self-correction from within each media institution, a way to preserve and protect the company, the press, and the public simultaneously.

It is interesting to consider Reuters' reaction to the onslaught—against both the news business and the truth itself—coming from Washington. On September 18, 2017, Reuters editor in chief Steven Adler introduced a project called "The Trump Effect: Tracking the Impact of the President's Policies." He wrote, "Shortly after Donald J. Trump became U.S. president last January, I wrote a memo to the Reuters staff providing guidance on how to cover the new Administration. The gist was that we should proceed as we would with any leader in the world, whether that leader admired journalists or viewed them as the enemy. That meant trying not to take sides or to make ourselves the story but rather to work dispassionately on behalf of Reuters users, who would need honest, carefully sourced, vigorous reporting on what this presidency meant for them." He continued by explaining that the Trump Effect would present hard data, video and text stories, and interactive graphics that would demonstrate—for better or worse—prevailing administration policies. The project has a dedicated website and is available to anyone, free of charge. The Trump Effect may be the closest thing the US (and the rest of the world) has to a single source of unbiased American political news.

In early 2018, I was unhappy to learn that the board of the Thomson Reuters Corporation had voted to approve a strategic partnership with the private equity firm Blackstone, which would entail Reuters selling Blackstone a 55 percent majority stake in its Financial & Risk unit. In the filing submitted to the US Securities and Exchange Commission, the details of the venture included the makeup of a new consociation: "The new partnership will be managed by a 10-person board composed of five representatives from the Investors and four from Thomson Reuters. The President and CEO of the new partnership will serve as a non-voting member of the board following the closing of the transaction. At the closing of the proposed transaction, F&R and Reuters will sign a 30-year agreement for Reuters to supply news and editorial content to the new partnership. Under the agreement, F&R will pay Reuters a minimum of US$325 million annually. For the duration of the news contract, Thomson Reuters will grant F&R a license to permit F&R to brand its information feeds and products/services with the 'Reuters' mark."

I had a fairly bad first impression of the Blackstone deal, and was not apprised of how it developed. I see private equity firms like Blackstone as slaughterhouses. They are designed to seek companies that are not well managed, that cannot exploit their own potential, or are floundering for some other reason. A company like that is a sitting duck if a private equity firm goes after it. Thomson Reuters indicated that they would use some of the purchase price from Blackstone to pay off an estimated $3 billion of debt and would use the lion's share of the remaining money to "repurchase shares via a substantial issuer/bid/tender offer made to all common shareholders." While I understand the lure of the deal when the money is on the table, it is one's attitude toward the future that ultimately determines how to proceed. If that attitude is pessimistic, with no courage and belief in the future, going with the money on the table is the next step. But if the attitude is confident, with an entrepreneurial spirit that is encouraged by Blackstone's interest, then the next step is to garner sufficient confidence to reject the offer and secure a loan to pay down the debt. I believed Thomson Reuters should have had that confidence. Apparently, they did not.

I was relieved when I learned the specifics of the deal, which make it very clear that the ownership of Reuters is still within Thomson Reuters. Technically, what Blackstone is doing is leasing the use of Reuters' news and editorial content. The term of this lease is thirty years, which might as well be an eternity. But nonetheless, the ownership has not been ceded to Blackstone, which is what I originally feared was the case. Reuters remains in charge of managing the news, and Blackstone cannot change or manipulate it. We shall see how it goes. But I don't like it.

In the face of overwhelming global pessimism (and growing cynicism), I nonetheless remain optimistic about the future. In taking a reckoning of the power for good, it is clear that sometimes a single force is enough to accomplish a Herculean task. In the case of the Watergate cover-up, uncovering the tentacles that snaked through the White House and reached all the way to the Oval Office—the force of the Washington Post was enough. But it was not a legacy of righting wrongs that gave the Post its power—it was the active support and guidance of Katharine Graham and her editor in chief, Ben Bradlee, both of whom were steadfast in their requirement that Woodward and Bernstein uphold the highest journalistic standards, and who were unflinching in their courage in publishing the results of their reporters' investigation, in spite of the exceptional potential for negative backlash.

In the final pages of *Castro and Stockmaster*, Michael Nelson writes, "Pehr Gyllenhammar had acquired for the trustees a standing which was unthinkable when I worked for the Company. Reuters was fortunate that, when Thomson sought to buy Reuters, the Chairman of Trustees was a man of such vision as Pehr Gyllenhammar, who had become Chairman in 1999... I derived some satisfaction from the fact that I had introduced Gyllenhammar to the Reuter family."

Having put in twenty-seven years as a member of that Reuter family, I can think of no more welcome validation than the suggestion that my own affinity for integrity affected Reuters in the same way that they affected me. It is a privilege to have worn the mantle of principle for so long, and if I have passed that mantle on to someone else, then all that I hoped to accomplish at Reuters has come to pass. I hope the next generation of directors will be able to say the same.

CHAPTER TWO

Heritage

Heritage *(n): c. 1200, "that which may be inherited," from Old French iritage, eritage, heritage "heir; inheritance, ancestral estate, heirloom," from heriter "inherit," from Late Latin hereditare, ultimately from Latin heres (genitive heredis) "heir" (see heredity). Meaning "condition or state transmitted from ancestors" is from 1620s.*

—Oxford English Dictionary

On a brisk day in October in the year 1658, a fleet of forty-five Swedish warships sailed south from Stockholm toward the narrow Oresund Sound on Denmark's northern coast. Aboard one of the ships was a middle-aged peasant farmer named Mans Andersson—a man I know virtually nothing about other than the fact that he left his home in Smaland to fight the Danish on behalf of the Swedish crown, and that he would become the first of my ancestors to have the Gyllenhammar name joined to his own.

Sweden's national registry and genealogical records are among the most comprehensive of any nation, and like many old families, the long line of my Gyllenhammar ancestors is well documented. Occasionally I am asked if I feel a sense of identification or commonality with these earlier generations. My first inclination is to dismiss this kind of personal identification with one's ancestors as a flight of fancy. Nonetheless, it is impressive to contemplate the collective scope of the Gyllenhammars' work and accomplishments. One common thread in the family is extensive military service, and other Gyllenhammar vocations over many generations include tanner, legislator, farmer, hunting master, carpenter, police inspector, painter/sculptor, pastry chef, railway engineer, pharmacist, dentist, and composer. This speaks to a broad array of sensibilities from the artistic and intellectual to the athletic and mechanical. It's now generally accepted that there is a genetic factor at play in determining whether one will excel at music or math, or whether one will be drawn to mechanical disciplines or agriculture. According to some studies, there is even a link between genes and the tolerance (or lack thereof) of dishonesty. So, I suppose I could say that I identify with my ancestors indirectly, through the catholic scope of their qualities, and for the integrity implicit in their inclination toward service of their country.

As a child, I was aware—through various anecdotes and family lore recounted by my parents—of having come from a definitive place, and of roots that were clearly identified in well-documented family trees. My mother was Jewish, the child of Russian-born Mathias Kaplan and Sara Friedman Kaplan, who emigrated to Sweden from Frankfurt. Most of my maternal grandmother's relatives remained in Germany, where it is believed they were virtually eradicated by the Nazis during the Holocaust. I was very aware of and influenced by all three of those cultural distinctions in my household—the Swedish, Anglo-Scottish, and Jewish. My mother's sister Irma had traveled to Berlin in 1933 and during her visit there she understood what the future in Hitler's Germany held for Jews. I have no memories of my Aunt Irma talking to my parents about the signs of impending catastrophe that were plain for anyone to see in Berlin, but I do know that both of my parents were deeply affected by and fearful of what Irma told them.

I don't recall my mother often speaking of her lost family in later years after the war, but the importance of keeping their memories alive was understood. If we did not remember, who would? Many years later when I was an adult, I wrote to the German Federal Archives (or Bundesarchiv) seeking information about my mother's family. In due time I received a reply in the form of a list. There were my mother's family's names, one after the other, each name followed by categorized listings for "Deportation," "Date of Death," and "Place of Death." From that document, I learned that almost all of them lost their lives in one of three concentration camps: Theresienstadt, Dachau, and Auschwitz. What was accomplished by my obtaining this chilling and meticulously recorded postmortem? The finality and validity of those names, those details cataloged with such clinical precision. To have that small reckoning, to see each name, each year, each place. So that they are not forgotten.

On my father's side, several branches of our family originated in Scotland, including the Setons and the Erskines. They were an esteemed set. The Highland Seton Clan boasted a royal connection by virtue of Alexander, Lord Seton, who married the sister of King Robert the Bruce. The Gyllenhammars are also kin to the Bruce-allied Clan Erskine, whose noble origins dated back to the thirteenth century, and whose fortunes failed in the eighteenth century with the fallout caused by John Erskine's participation in the Jacobite uprising. One of the disgraced Erskines was sent to

Gothenburg to learn a trade, and he settled there for a number of years. He seems to have found Gothenburg dull enough to merit his founding a private billiards club there, and the club has withstood the test of time. Two hundred fifty years later, it is still possible to shoot pool in the Royal Bachelor's Club or to enjoy a drink in the Large Club Room where Erskine's portrait hangs over the fireplace.

George Seton found his way from Scotland to Sweden as well, settling near Stockholm in the eighteenth century. Seton apparently wished to live like a king, as he bought the royal Ekolsund Castle from King Gustav III in 1785, and from that time forward the castle was occupied by Setons for the next 125 years. In hindsight it is interesting that so many of our Scottish ancestors lived so nearby in Sweden. But it is our direct line of descent from the old Swedish Gyllenhammar line—and its origins in war, patriotic service, and monarchical recognition—that remains the best documented and known to me.

Our ancestral family patriarch Mans Andersson was born in the early seventeenth century at a time when Sweden was reaching the apex of an unprecedented era of political and military power. This time period is often referred to as the *stormaktstid*, a Swedish word that translates as the "age of great power." Young King Gustav II Adolph, enthroned in 1611 when he was just fifteen years old, was an outspoken Protestant with a passion for education and a military prowess that would be viewed historically as a form of genius. The Golden King (as he was called) had no personal or political motivation to take up the gauntlet of the Thirty Years' War—a series of regional conflicts in which virtually every major power in Europe had a stake. But the conflicts pitted Catholics against Protestants, and the Golden King was deeply concerned about the fate of the Protestant population in present-day

Germany, who faced possible eradication without the intervention of a powerful ally.

Sweden's empire at the time was comprised of a large stretch of coastland forming a horseshoe around the Baltic Sea, and included present-day Finland, parts of Denmark and Norway, and northern Germany, making Sweden the preeminent power in Europe. King Gustav had nothing to gain by lending the power of a Swedish alliance to the German Protestants, and no motivation to do so other than the agitation of his own conscience. Sweden's Lutheran church was under no threat. The Peace of Augsburg of 1555 had established the principle *cuius regio, eius religio*—whose realm, his religion. Quite simply, a prevailing ruler would dictate the religion over the dominion in his control. Catholic ruler, Catholic state. Protestant ruler, Lutheran state. But it applied only to Lutheran Protestantism. The Calvinists of the Habsburg-ruled Kingdom of Bohemia were unprotected by this realm-religion principle.

Upholding his fabled moral code, the Golden King chose in 1632 to put his life at risk and personally led an army to Bohemia to fight on behalf of the Protestants. The well-beloved King Gustav and his forces prevailed, and he won the battle, but at the cost of his own life—making it the ultimate Pyrrhic victory. The Thirty Years' War came to a close fifteen years later, and the remaining hostilities that would ebb and flow for the latter half of the century in northern Europe were largely a prolonged wrangle over territory.

The regional tug-of-war between Denmark and Sweden dates back to the fourteenth century, when the Kalmar Union bound Sweden to both Norway and the dominant nation of Denmark. In 1523, the self-declared King Gustav declared Sweden's independence and severed its ties with the Holy Roman Empire, and by extension with Catholicism. The remaining Danish southern provinces of the Scandinavian peninsula were ceded to Sweden in 1658, as part of a territorial acquisition dictated by the Treaty of Roskilde. For peasants like Mans Andersson, who were the latest in a long line of ancestors living and farming in or near the Scania region, it is likely that their sense of loyalty to Denmark-Norway was not necessarily so quickly forgotten, and that some continued to consider themselves more Danish than Swedish. Just five months before Mans Andersson and his son Jonas answered the call to join the Swedish fleet in the Battle of Oresund, the inhabitants of Bornholm, a small island some eighty miles west of the Danish Coast, successfully revolted against the Swedish Crown, returning the territory to Danish rule. Considering these recent events, it is easier to understand why the willingness of men like Mans and Jonas Andersson to join the Swedish naval fight at Oresund engendered real gratitude from the Crown.

The saltwater Strait of Oresund separates Sweden from Denmark and provides a crucial connective passage between the Baltic Sea to the Kattegat Strait and the Atlantic Ocean. This maritime Atlantic-Baltic conduit is the sine qua non of strategic positions in the Baltic regions and was (and today still is) one of the most important shipping lanes in the world, heavily trafficked with vessels laden with grain, iron, copper, timber, tar, hemp, and furs. From any standpoint—military, economic, or political—unhindered access to the Oresund was imperative. Any force that obtained sole control of the strait effectively wielded the ultimate power and authority in all regional matters of trade and travel. It was therefore in the interest of every prevailing European power to prevent any single nation-state from ever controlling both the north and south coasts of the Oresund again. If each coast were controlled by a different nation-state, it lessened the chances that the passage would be politically leveraged or weaponized. The Treaty of Roskilde transferred ownership of the southern Scandinavian peninsula from Denmark to Sweden. The local resident may have been unhappy about their sudden and compulsory allegiance to the Swedish Crown, but the powers of continental Europe would have found the prospect of a Swedish Scania more palatable and less threatening that that of a Danish Scania.

So the tangled web of centuries of shifting alliances and hostilities continued to play themselves out between Sweden and Denmark, and in the fall of 1658 the subject of dispute was control of the Strait of Oresund. Under the command of Lord High Admiral Carl Gustaf Wrangel, the Swedish fleet's mission was simple—support their army's siege of Copenhagen by blocking Denmark's access to naval resupply and trade vessels. Denmark's occasional ally, the Dutch United Provinces, sent a squadron of their own to engage the Swedish ships. Denmark badly needed this assistance. The Dutch ships were in a position to take advantage of strong northern winds, but those same winds effectively prohibited Denmark's seven warships from leaving their Copenhagen port, leaving the Swedes and the Dutch to duke it out alone.

The Dutch painter Willem van de Velde witnessed the ensuing clash and documented what he saw in his painting *The Battle of the Sound.* I know nothing of the details of Mans Andersson's onboard role, nor do I know how he met his death. But van de Velde's painting gives a very vivid sense of what the battle was like. In the monochrome rendering, a sixty-gun Swedish warship is in the foreground firing upon a Dutch vessel, identified as the Dutch commander's warship *Eendracht.* Off its starboard side, a smaller ship is sinking; tiny figures are visible as they leap into the water and wave to an overcrowded lifeboat. Tall-masted ships fill the field of view in every direction, the horizon papered with overlapping sails as thick columns of smoke from firing cannons and burning boats rise into the sky. In the distance, the rounded turrets of Kronborg Castle are visible on the Danish coast. The scene looks chaotic and loud, and the violence occurring in close quarters—to the men on board one ship firing on another, the destruction and carnage would be immediately audible and visible on a very human level.

The powerful currents surging through the sound severely limited the ships' maneuverability, and the fighting was fierce and at very close range. Four Swedish ships were captured, and the Dutch successfully drove the remainder of the fleet from the sound. Of Sweden's 6,000 men, over 400 were dead, 650 wounded, and hundreds captured. Among the Swedish casualties was Mans Andersson, officially listed as a captain from the province of Smaland's Jonkoping regiment, along with one of his sons. A second son, Jonas, survived the battle, and returned home to his family with the heavy heart of one who has paid the price of warfare with his dearest blood, but who has also gained something highly prized by his kinsmen—honor.

Like most residents in southern Sweden's Smaland, Andersson's family were peasant farmers who settled on the floodplains of fertile soil and arable land when the Scandinavian glacier retreated to the north circa 11,000 BC. The earliest settlers were hunters and fishers who soon evolved to cultivate farming skills and animal husbandry. By the sixteenth century Sweden had been a primarily agricultural region for centuries, and the Andersson family would have been accustomed to the area's periodic crop failures and long harsh winters. Life for landed peasant families like the Anderssons was physically challenging, particularly in the grain-harvesting months of August and September when families could expect to work twenty-hour days. In the community of village and extended families, the Andersson family would have made the winter hours more passable by communal meals, fireside conversation, and the consumption of aquavit—homemade grain or potato-based alcohol vilified by one Swedish king as the ruination of the Swedish people. Seventeenth-century Smaland is also notable as the region in which Swedish witch mania first erupted—from 1668 to 1676—fifteen years before the infamous Salem witch trials in America's Massachusetts.

In Scanian peasant culture of that time, personal honor was valued above all other qualities, and loss of one's honorable reputation could result in ostracization from community—a punishment that was nothing less than the severance of a lifeline. In the sixteenth century, the Swedish King Gustav Vasa had ended compulsory military conscription, so that "the native peasantry may sit at home, tend their fields and meadows, feed their wives and children, and no longer go out to get themselves killed." By Mans Andersson's lifetime, the Golden King had devised new rules of conscription, and King Charles X Gustav made it clear that more was needed and expected of peasant families. When Denmark declared war on Sweden in 1657, county governors received word from the Swedish Council alerting them of the imminent war and asking them to do their part in bolstering the courage of their constituents and encouraging them to actively partake in the defense of the fatherland. In instances where King Charles X Gustav specifically requested that a county governor muster the unit of volunteers, the response was negotiated and agreed upon by the peasants themselves. But after many successive calls for volunteer soldiers, numbers and patience were growing thin. When a new request for the mustering of volunteer soldiers reached counties in the autumn of 1658, the Crown met with somewhat more resistance and found many fewer men stepping forward to answer the call. For that reason, the willing participation of men from families such as that of Mans Andersson was especially appreciated by the Crown.

In recognition of the honor and sacrifice of Mans Andersson's service and death in the Battle of the Sound, he was posthumously knighted as *Adliga ätter* (untitled nobility) and introduced at the *Riddarhuset*—the Swedish House of Nobility—in 1668. With a family's ennoblement, the Crown also presented them with a new name, and from that time onward the recipient would cease using the patronymic system and instead pass the noble surname down to each successive generation. These names were generally crafted to impart an imposing or admirable air—the one bestowed upon Andersson and his descendants at the *Riddarhuset* was Gyllenhammar—which translates as golden battle axe. A perusal of a list of 2,350 numbered noble family names produces eighty-one surnames with the golden prefix "gyllen," including Gyllenpistol (golden gun), Gyllensvard (golden sword), Gyllengranat (golden grenade), Gyllenskold (golden skull), and the impressive if nautically dubious Gyllenskepp (golden ship). Other popular prefixes of the time were Silfver (silver) and the Germanic Adler and Ehren—meaning eagle and honor respectively.

In my childhood, there was little novelty in our name, and I felt no compunction to live up to the golden battle axe family standard. The Gyllenhammar lineage of nobility was a historical fact, but not a source of self-importance—on the contrary, my father was a very modest man who had no patience for ostentation or self-aggrandizing of any kind. My father was an insurance company executive, and my mother a pianist. I had one sibling—my sister, Anne, who was four and a half years my senior. We lived in a comfortable flat in Gothenburg, the rooms often filled with piano music as my mother played and practiced daily.

As young children, my sister and I were encouraged to be intellectually curious and to speak our minds—ours was the sort of family that preferred lively discourse at the dinner table over silence. Some of my earliest memories are of that sense of unease I associate with my Aunt Irma's warnings about the atmosphere in Berlin. When the war broke out, I remember almost nothing but being evacuated to my great-uncle's country home, owing to the expected German bombardment of Gothenburg. Like the much larger Pied Piper operation in London, children in geographically vulnerable cities like Gothenburg were relocated to rural areas in Sweden, as were some 70,000 Finnish children. My days in my great-uncle Oskar's home were happy ones, and I grew deeply fond of him. Oskar Gyllenhammar was a lovely man and a very successful and interesting person.

Born in 1866 on the Gotland Island in the Baltic Sea, some sixty miles from Sweden's southeastern coastline, Oskar Leopold Gyllenhammar began his career as a bookkeeper and office manager of the Ystad Sugar Refinery and was later a member of the Board of the Nordic Trade Bank 1917–1925. His biography in a Swedish collection of historical business profiles also lists him as founder of the Scandinavian letter pigeon union. But he is best known for his invention of a rapid-cooking porridge that made him the effective founder of the Swedish instant oatmeal industry as we know it. I was too young to be impressed by my great-uncle's business success or prosperity—though I do recall feeling the silver tea he always drank was a notable beverage, I think what drew me to him at the outset was his capacity for listening. When I talked to him, he gave me his full attention, as one would with an adult, rather than listening as a kind of patient concession to a child. Even after we returned home to Gothenburg, I continued to visit him each week and always looked forward to spending a pleasant hour in conversation as he sipped his silver tea.

My father did not quite share my high esteem of Oskar. He thought Oskar was vain—and perhaps he was, though I do not recall him that way. My father was an enormously modest man, one who shied away from publicity and accolades, and as such he had no tolerance for vanity in others. He was also a person of enormous integrity, independent of thought, well read and well spoken. I admired him, but also differed from him in many ways. Even in my childhood I was determinedly independent as to how I wanted things done, a trait that often resulted in his disapproval. But we had some common ground as well. I inherited his great love for the sea, and like him, my affinity for sailing and racing boats began early in childhood. My father could not afford to buy a sailboat of his own until after the war, and even then, it was not a particularly flashy vessel, but it was sound, reliable, and unobtrusively seaworthy, not prone to accidents or liable to stray off course—rather like my father himself.

My parents had a true love match, which was perhaps more the exception than the rule in those days. I remember their frequent hushed-voice discussions during the war, and of being acutely aware as the war broke out of my father's fear for my Jewish mother and her family. I'm sure that in part his fear was due to the fact that in spite of its official neutrality, Sweden was in reality accommodating the Nazis by allowing German military transports to travel through Sweden (often by use of their railroad system) and by continuing to export its iron ore to Germany—a crucial element in the manufacturing of German weaponry. Sweden's willingness to indulge in this level of cooperation with the Nazis gave rise to the reasonable fear that the degree of difference between accommodating the enemy and colluding with the enemy was small. Sweden could well have been a few simple steps from espousing that fascism. My father thought—both then and later in life—that it was scandalous that Sweden had not only stayed out of the war rather than assisting the Allied powers, but also allowed those Nazi convoys through the southern Scandinavian peninsula to German-occupied Norway.

I was happy and relieved when the war finally came to an exhausted end, eager for life to return to normal in spite of the fact that the prewar state of things was less than a hazy memory, as I had been just four when Germany invaded Poland. I believe on some level I understood that things could never return to the way they had been before the war. The sense of unease I had always felt about my own country—which had its genesis in my early childhood listening to my parents talk about the war—never left me. From my childhood on I harbored a fear that there might be a fascist tendency in Sweden that was buried just below the politely neutral surface. And as a Jewish boy, I had seen just how barbaric that kind of fascism could be. It was little wonder my father had been so fearful for my mother. In the agonizing months after Germany's surrender, one after another of my mother's family was declared dead, slaughtered in concentration camps. I can recall hearing only of a single survivor—a cousin who had gone to France to work for Radio Free Europe.

Life went on in Sweden after the war, as it did in the rest of Europe. But I would never forget what I had seen and heard, nor did I ever shake the feeling that the cool and politic veneer of a civilized and humanistic Sweden was a flimsy camouflage at best. I had recognized what one could call the truth of my Swedish heritage from those early moments of my childhood. I understood that what was solid ground for me as a young person could change—that beneath the strata of security and permanence there would always be movement. Passive underground rumbling—the kind my parents sensed with Sweden's accommodation of the Nazis—could in the future erupt without warning into a violent quake into fascism that could leave the national landscape and everything Sweden purported to be unrecognizable.

The nature of a solid place, of the ground of national identity, is tectonic. I think this is a difficult idea for many to accept—the inevitability of upheaval in one's own back yard. It is an idea with which I imagine my ancestor Mans Andersson was much more comfortable. In those generations, war with Denmark came and went, over and over again. Catholicism, the Hanseatic League, and the Black Death dominated until they dwindled, and the Swedish Empire grew fat until the pendulum began to swing back, and it was starved to the bone. In the Sweden of Mans Andersson, the triumph of the *stormaktstid* and the tragedy of the Golden King's death would have been celebrated and mourned with the resolute acceptance of people who were long accustomed to the historical cycles of gain and loss, people who did not always insert a sense of self into the concept of losing a thing or leaving a place.

Perhaps it is that ancient equanimity that is my strongest link to the earliest Gyllenhammars. Having absorbed and internalized my father's fearfulness during wartime, I may have made my peace with the specter of change. In the decades that followed I developed a fine-tuned sensor for the shifting of plates beneath a solid surface, and a pragmatic attitude about upheaval and departure. It is accepted without saying that structural integrity is crucial to human well-being—and yet the laws of physics dictate that solid and firm structures degrade over time, and orderly systems such as corporations, democracies, and nations grow disorderly. So I learned at an early age that once I could no longer maintain my footing and stand upright in my workplace, or a partnership, or the organizations I helped run, or my nation itself, then I did not hesitate to leave. Whether it was a home, or a career, or even a country, I knew when the moment had arrived when things were beginning to shift and integrity had been lost. And when integrity was lost, it was time to move on to solid ground elsewhere, and I did so again and again without hesitation, or any compulsion to look back with regret.

CHAPTER THREE

Innovation

Innovation *(n) mid-15c., "restoration, renewal," from Late Latin innovationem (nominative innovatio), noun of action from past participle stem of innovare "to change; to renew" (see innovate). Meaning "a novel change, experimental variation, new thing introduced in an established arrangement".*

–Oxford English Dictionary

I am not a person who finds any value in looking at the past to ruminate over what should have been, or what might have been. Nonetheless, beginnings are important, as are all of the triumphs and travails that emanate from them. Aristotle famously said, "the whole is greater than the sum of its parts," and that is very true, but nonetheless, the sum of a life's parts is a necessary calculation.

In reflecting on what has been formative my own life, I consider the consequential parts not to be things or titles, but people. When a company or an organization has been the most rewarding, it has always been due to the people that the company or organization brought into my sphere, people I had the privilege of getting to know. That is certainly true of my time at Volvo, and it is true of my time in Sweden itself.

I spent my first fifty-eight years living in Sweden full-time, much of it in Gothenburg. On graduating from the University of Lund in 1959, I married my college sweetheart Christina Engellau, who had also grown up in Gothenburg and was the daughter of Volvo chairman Gunnar Engellau. I got a job at the Amphion Insurance Company in Gothenburg and remained there for several years before my father asked me to join him at the Skandia Insurance Company in Stockholm. I ultimately succeeded him as CEO of the company.

My father's request surprised me. He had never been of the belief that executives should promote the employment of their own family members—in fact he was very resistant to the idea. But the company chairman asked him directly about the prospect of bringing me on board, and he ultimately agreed and offered me a starting position as an assistant administrative manager. The job involved our family moving from Gothenburg to Stockholm, a prospect that Christina was enthusiastic about, since it would allow her to achieve a little distance from her family. I remember her father reacting to the news of my joining Skandia by saying, "I would never engage anyone at Volvo who is related to me."

I was baffled, therefore, when just eighteen months later my father-in-law (by way of his then chairman of the board) approached me and asked to have a conversation about the possibility of my going to work at Volvo. I could not help but think that the job would be truly fascinating. What possible reason could I have for saying no? The only person who mattered to me with an objection was my wife. Christina loved living our independent life in Stockholm, and she was now facing the possibility that the man she had married was a de facto crown prince, positioned as her father's successor, which meant moving back to Gothenburg. I knew it was not what Christina wanted, but she put on a brave face and agreed that I take the job at Volvo, and that we and our four children would leave Stockholm.

There were a few articles written at the time, making reference to my employment and family connections at Skandia and Volvo, and suggesting those connections as the reason for hiring me at Volvo, but as none were able to back up those insinuations with factual reports to demonstrate that my professional skills and competence were insufficient, that sort of chatter died away quickly. My new colleagues at Volvo also overcame their surprise, as I was considerably younger than the average top man at any company—and they easily adjusted to my new position. From the very first, I loved both the job and the company. I found it challenging and exciting in the best of ways. I was tough with management—and while I had no desire to do a symbolic house-clearing, I did replace those I felt inadequate for the job, and worked closely with those who had potential, trying to make them real partners in the company.

I vividly remember going down to the Volvo plant for the first time to visit and talk to the workers. It was only very rarely that the workers saw a CEO or top management walking the factory floor, and in those occurrences the executive would be more ingratiating than businesslike, dressed down in something deemed sufficiently casual for the workers' sensibilities. I arrived on the factory floor still in my suit and tie and addressed them directly, with questions to which I genuinely wanted to know the answers—I was asking them to share knowledge and expertise that I knew only they had. My approach seemed to resonate with the workers, because they welcomed me with surprise and genuine warmth. Over the years, my visits to the factory floor were among the parts of my job I most looked forward to.

By some accounts the genesis of Sweden's automotive future was conceived in 1924 over a large dish of red crayfish at a popular Stockholm restaurant. It was there that Assar Gabrielsson—sales manager for the SFK industrial company—and SFK engineer Gustaf Larson—happened to run into one another. They jointly tucked into the crustaceans—which had been boiled in beer and seasoned with fresh dill—eating them cold from the shell. During the course of that meal the conversation turned to cars, namely the 15,000 vehicles being imported into Sweden annually. Was it not possible to produce cars locally, they wondered? As Gabrielsson would later write, "Swedish steel was good, but Swedish roads were bad." The two began discussing the possibility of designing and building a quintessentially Swedish automobile, designed to safely withstand the rigors of northern European winters and Swedish roads, and constructed to the highest standards of quality and safety. Three years later, in April of 1927, the first Volvo car rolled out of the Lundby factory gates—the ÖV 4, nicknamed Jakob. The ÖV 4 (short for Öppen Vagn 4 cylindrar) was an open four-seater with a four-cylinder engine, with leather upholstery, and a deep blue chassis with black fenders atop twenty-inch wheels with wooden spokes.

On the fiftieth anniversary of Jakob's arrival on the scene, we published a Volvo Jubilee historical booklet that celebrated the history of what Volvo had accomplished in the last half century. It opened with a brief essay on the ÖV 4 that began, "It's 1927, a year of superlatives. Lindbergh flies the Atlantic...movies talk... Babe Ruth hits 60 home runs. A year of automobiles, too. Ford is phasing out the Model T... names like Packard, Willys-Overland, Reo, Pierce-Arrow, Stutz, Auburn are all strong in the American market. There's a worldwide fascination with automobiles. In Sweden, a new name enters the field...Volvo. A 4-cylinder open touring car called Jakob, begins what is to become the outstanding example of constant progress through evolution in the automotive industry."

The war years were difficult for Volvo, but the company rebounded, and by the 1960s was boasting healthy car sales and exports, and producing trucks and buses, as well as jet turbines for the Swedish Air Force. When I arrived, I found the company to be in very good shape. It was 1970, a year before the recession, and four years before the oil crisis that would impact the auto industry all over the world. The company's financials were more than sound, and in all respects Volvo had prospered in over two decades under the guidance of my father-in-law, Gunnar Engellau, who came to that position having been the engineer heading Volvo's aviation subsidiary.

Gustaf Larson wrote "Cars are driven by people. The guiding principle behind everything we make, therefore, is and must remain safety." When my father-in-law succeeded Assar Gabrielsson as Volvo's CEO, he elevated the concept of safety as a brand asset—something that differentiated it from every other automobile maker. I have great respect for my predecessors, particularly my father-in-law, who was a great supporter of mine. I made many mistakes, but he never once told me he regretted picking me to succeed him, and I'm always touched when I think about that. But in order to keep Volvo evolving, I knew there must always be change, even when the current status quo was profitable. I believed we could take the brand asset of safety farther—by, among other things, extending the reflection of our consumer's values to our factory workers, by placing an emphasis on worker safety and well-being as well as on environmental issues. And I had some very specific ideas about the product development of cars, as well.

These ideas became the genesis of the Volvo 240 series, successor of the 140 and of the wildly popular Amazon model. The Volvo 240 would not be substantially changed in shape, but in technology it was totally different. Beginning from the base of a concept car known as VESC, the Volvo Experimental Safety Car, the 240 was distinguished from its predecessor with the addition of the newest B21 engine, specially designed struts and rack and pinion steering, large front and rear crumple zones, and oversize aluminum bumpers. The solidity and resilience of its chassis was extraordinary, and the 240 became the most robust passenger car on the market. Of course, safety remained the single top priority in every design decision, and it was evident that the 240 was the pinnacle of what could be achieved when the US used it to establish required safety standards for all American-made cars. I was able to say with full confidence at a ceremony celebrating the 240 that we had "...the world's safest car, one of the most worthwhile cars to buy, and a car that is already living legend and will be even more of one in the years to come."

Another avenue of change that I pursued was the relationship of our industry to the environment. In the early 1970s, the awareness of environmentalism was only beginning to rise, and in 1972, the very first global environmental convocation—the United Nations Environmental Conference—was organized to take place in Stockholm. I gave a keynote speech at that conference, and Volvo's website today still bears a line from it: "We are part of the problem—but we are also a part of the solution." It was a very deliberate choice of words on my part. These were very early days for environmentalism—it was just a few years after the formation of the Club of Rome—and it was not a popular subject in industry. I felt it was very important to avoid any ambivalent statements that could be construed as a denial that Volvo was a contributor to pollution and processes that were unfriendly to the environment. I wasn't going to claim that we were different, that we were the good ones. Instead, I admitted that we were bad too, and that needed to change. Why should it be so unheard of to admit the undeniable and take accountability for it?

Another new direction for Volvo was our participation in the development and production of space flight technology. In 1975, the European Space Agency was formed, a cooperative venture of twenty-two member-states. Volvo produced a component of the first Ariane rocket, a series of launchable spacecraft that were a collaborative project of Western Europe. I was not in attendance at the liftoff, as I was at a meeting with President Mitterrand and Chancellor Schmidt to present the project and its development to journalists in Paris. But I vividly remember seeing the liftoff on television, and watching the rocket rise from the launchpad into the sky. It was a very exciting moment.

One of the primary arenas for making the socially and humanistic oriented changes I prioritized was Volvo's assembly plants, beginning with the Kalmar factory, established in 1974, and later with the Uddevalla plant. The goal was to design plants around the supposition that employees should be able to find meaning and satisfaction in their work, and to work in a healthful and pleasing environment while neglecting neither efficiency nor economic results. As Åke Sandberg put it in Enriching Production, the project was "innovative, productive, and humane...with various concepts of group work." In developing the design and concepts, I worked with Volvo management and engineers and with the local and national unions to have an unfiltered source of information about what would truly benefit the workers.

In the Kalmar plant, we created a work-batch system to move away from the single-repetitive task assembly line system. Groups of workers were formed into teams, and each team was responsible for the collective assembly of one of the car's systems. In a 1987 article in the *New York Times*, Steve Lohr cited the positive effect of the Kalmar plant on Volvo's rising productivity and quality, and of the benefits of a work-batch team approach over an assembly line approach, writing, "Because each worker typically performs a series of tasks, the 'cycle times'—or the period the worker has to complete his assignment—are often several minutes instead of the several seconds common on the assembly line. In addition, the workers in a team are taught to do several jobs, not only to escape monotony but also to fill in for sick or vacationing workers."

Kalmar was the breakthrough I had hoped it would be. It became a workplace in which human-centered designs and concepts created improved jobs, which led to improved worker well-being and productivity. In conceiving the next plant, Uddevalla, the basic Kalmar concept remained, but was refined to be a bit more radical and sophisticated. The assembly line production system was dispensed with altogether at Uddevalla in favor of a fixed-site car assembly system in which multiple teams of skilled laborers worked in cooperation to collectively assemble entire vehicles. Åke Sandberg described a visit to Uddevalla in which he observed "the human orientation of the work being done...a group of nine workers assembled a car from beginning to end. They conferred with each other while working, resulting in the completion of the entire car before the morning coffee break. This team like all others in the plant had no supervisor. And the first level manager of this and the seven other teams in the product workshop was on vacation; the groups could clearly manage their own work."

My work along these lines of reinventing the labor model drew interest from others in the automotive industry, and many came to visit the factories. In 1973 and 1974, we hosted visits from Henry Ford II and Leonard Woodcock, the latter then president of the United Auto Workers union. I came to know and like both of these men enormously. Ford loved the Kalmar plant, and told me, "Pehr, this is a revolution!" Leonard Woodcock was also impressed with Kalmar's humanization of the labor system. It was an issue that had long been of concern to him. Ten years prior to his visit to Kalmar, a 1964 *New York Times* article reported the UAW's refusal to drop demands for better conditions in return for an improved financial package. The article stated, "Leonard Woodcock, UAW vice president and director of the General Motors Department, said at a news conference today that he had no illusions that the workers 'can be bought off this time' on working conditions. 'Our purpose this year is to humanize conditions in the General Motors plants,' he said."

Woodcock himself was truly a great humanist. He loved people. And I found him to be an extraordinary person in many ways. His visit to the Kalmar plant was the first time I had the occasion to meet him, and I thought he was very different from most of the union bosses I had encountered. He was very much admired in many circles and had an excellent reputation with the union members. At that time, he ranked ninth on the infamous "Nixon Enemies List," which to me is a fact that in and of itself made for a solid endorsement of his character and integrity.

Leonard and I started a dialogue after his Kalmar visit. He later came to visit me at my country home in the Swedish archipelago, and we became close friends. I found Leonard to be a human being with almost no prejudice, which I found unusual for a union leader. The scope of his social commitment and his professional aptitude was uniquely wide. He was a champion of civil rights who had marched with Martin Luther King Jr., and as Jimmy Carter's personal representative in Beijing, he successfully negotiated reestablishing US-China ties after a lapse of thirty years. Secretary of State Madeleine Albright called him a "distinguished leader and a trusted advisor to American presidents from Jimmy Carter to Bill Clinton," and said that "with patience, skill and a low-key style born of long, late-night sessions negotiating on behalf of America's working men and women, he helped guide the American and Chinese governments toward the establishment of ties that have well served the interests of our two peoples."

Leonard Woodcock was one of those rare people in power who both knew how to communicate very effectively and who was committed to using that ability to help where it was needed and create positive change. And he could do that because he was gifted with an innate sense of diplomacy—the kind that cannot be learned. The root of that diplomacy was an authentic empathy for people. Leonard said that those around him sometimes believed him to be aloof or emotionally cold, but I never did. He may have been reserved, but to those who knew him well, that reserve quickly gave way to great warmth and generosity. Leonard was born into a working-class family and never finished college, but his intuition for knowing what to say and how and when to say it elevated him to the very highest circles in both the labor and diplomatic arenas.

I was very lucky in terms of the people I met during that time, and with whom I developed friendships—truly exceptional individuals like Leonard, and Henry Ford, and Joseph Slater, who I believe I first met at that 1972 environmental conference in Stockholm. I am not exaggerating when I say that they were people through whom I saw hope for humanity, and at times I believe each of them also saw it through me. In an introduction for my book *People at Work*, Leonard wrote, "In an industrial world believing firmly in the economy of scale—bigger is beautiful—Mr. Gyllenhammar argues that there is a limit to the necessity and efficiency of large-sized factories. In a system relying increasingly on technology, he asserts that the machine is, after all, the creation of the human being and not vice versa. The conclusion to be drawn, therefore, is that work must be reorganized to suit people, and this in turn requires changing the technology that chains people to the machine."

Henry Ford II was also very taken with the Kalmar plant's innovation and the concept of reorganizing work to suit the human being. The Ford Motor Company had been associated with social responsibility as far back as 1914, when Henry Ford Senior famously decided to raise wages to five dollars a day, which for most of his workers amounted to a doubling of their paychecks. Ford wrote about his decision in his autobiography, saying, "We wanted to pay these wages so that the business would be on a lasting foundation. We were building for the future. A low wage business is always insecure."

This bold step in establishing what is now called an efficiency wage model to reduce turnover and increase worker morale and productivity was a remarkable success. In an NPR story, Sarah Cwiek reported that, "The benefits were almost immediate. Productivity surged, and the Ford Motor Company doubled its profits in less than two years. Ford ending up calling it the best cost-cutting move he'd ever made." And with the benefit of hindsight, some economists credit Ford's wage model as a galvanizing factor in the growth of a healthy middle class. His namesake and grandson, Henry Ford II, had undertaken a battle with him for control of the family business, and once he took control, the younger Ford masterminded a decade-long surge that took the company from the brink of bankruptcy to an industrial powerhouse, demonstrating the determination he shared with his grandfather to do the right thing for the family business.

Henry Ford II and I became good friends after his Kalmar trip, and I spent some time visiting with him the following year at the Ford Motor Company headquarters in Detroit. True to his reputation, Ford was a study in contradictions, and there were things about him I liked, and things I did not. He was straightforward and direct, an unapologetic capitalist who nonetheless understood the needs of both his management and his workers. I would say that he was probably a good—rather than a great—executive, but I had respect for the way he conducted his affairs and his company dedication, often working long, productive hours.

At the time of my Ford visit, Lee Iacocca was the company's CEO. Ford suggested we go over to his office to say hello, and I agreed. When Henry opened the door and saw Iacocca sitting with his feet up on his desk, he muttered, "Dammit, he's so badly educated it's unbelievable." We walked into the office, where Iacocca smiled and said "Hello, Pehr," still sitting with his feet propped on the desk. I'm not sure which irritated Henry Ford more—that he didn't take his feet down and stand when the boss entered the room, or that he addressed me by my first name when we'd never previously met. As we came out of Lee Iacocca's office, Henry shook his head and said, "Dammit, I'll fire him!" And though the record will reflect it had nothing to do with me, the very next day Ford did exactly that. It was later reported that when Iacocca asked why he was being fired, Ford replied, "I just don't like you."

Henry Ford was tremendously enthusiastic about what I had showed him at Volvo, and loved to discuss innovation and progress, but at the same time he was hesitant about doing what needed to be done to make that happen at Ford. He told me, "I've done nothing because the climate here is so awful, I can't make anything happen." I think it more accurate to say that Ford knew what needed to be done and how it needed to be done, but he was not as willing as I was to step outside of the status quo of society and accept the consequences that come with being labeled a rebel bent on change.

Most people are conservative at heart, and cling to the past as the model for the present—everything was better yesterday than it is now or will be tomorrow. Any change in civilization, in society, in manufacturing—or any module of present life—is threatened by new methods and approaches. So, when you innovate, you are met with suspicion—you are a threat to the present. And the lack of willingness to change is always a very difficult obstacle. Whenever you have a major change on the horizon, the effort will already be there to doom and defeat it. That is what I experienced firsthand, and I was amazed by it—you really had to fight for everything. And when a turnover occurs at the leadership level, there develops a bilious focus to undo the innovation of the predecessor, much as Donald Trump obsessively dismantled as much of Barack Obama's legislation as he could. And if I needed proof of that proclivity to cling to establishment, I had it when I left Volvo. In short order, the Uddevalla plant was shut down, and Kalmar was terminated the following year. Those things I had accomplished at Volvo that could be undone and dismantled were undone and dismantled.

For those who have an appetite for the minutiae of the events leading up to my departure from Volvo, they are certainly well documented in many places. A concise summary is that we were moving forward with a plan to merge with the French auto manufacturer Renault. But the deal was scuttled for Volvo by what the *New York Times* described as "a revolt from its own management." The 1993 article by Richard W. Stevenson reported that, "In a move apparently engineered by Soren Gyll, the Swedish company's No. 2 executive, Volvo's board canceled a meeting…at which the shareholders were to have voted on the merger."

And with that, I had had enough. It was not a question of personal pride, or an inability to withstand a failure (as I had done that twelve years earlier with the failure to get a qualified majority vote for a cooperative project with the Norwegian oil industry). The behind-the-scenes machinations to whittle away support for the merger were endemic of something larger—put simply, the lack of guts in the people around me—the unwillingness to take a stand. The backdoor maneuvering by executives who were too cowardly to stand on the podium and fight for what they wanted publicly sickened me. I had no stomach for commerce without conscience. I neither wanted nor asked for anything from Volvo to speed me on my way—I didn't want to speak my piece, or publicly call out the most notable of the plotters. And in spite of what was reported in the press and what some people still claim to this day, I did not ask for or receive a lucrative golden handshake. I was done, and that was that. I got myself out immediately, resigning my position.

I knew that Uddevalla and Kalmar would soon be in the corporate crosshairs. My successors made it clear that they had contrary views to mine. They were neither willing nor capable of supporting and continuing the effort required to run a plant in which one had to motivate, train, and educate people. There was, in my mind, an element of spite in their returning Volvo to the old, traditional way of manufacturing. As I saw it, they were essentially finding it favorable to return to the *Modern Times* mind-set of Charlie Chaplin, in which he portrayed the worker as a helpless cog in the wheel of merciless industry. But while doors that one has opened can be closed by others, and while innovations can be disposed of, history cannot be unwritten. The achievements at Kalmar and Uddevalla were real, with quantifiable results, and they were experienced directly by every worker employed at those plants. As Åke Sandberg writes in *Enriching Production*, there was great loss in closing down the plants: "But ideas of competitive and human-centred forms of industrial production are still alive and they are practiced in various sectors. The Volvo Kalmar and Uddevalla production concepts are still used, by academics and practitioners alike, as reference points and as reminders of the possibility of alternatives with quality in both work and products."

When it came time to close the door on Volvo after twenty-four years and move forward, I did so without hesitation, and never looked back with bitterness. Though I was in large part an outlier at Volvo who suffered the consequences of acting against the mainstream, I would push for the very same changes if I had to do it over again. I understand that many saw me simply as a rebel and a contrarian, but I believe I did some truly good things. The seventies and eighties were very exciting times, and in my privileged position at Volvo they afforded enormous opportunities for growth. My departure from Volvo (like my arrival) was never a zero-sum game. It was not an asset that was erased and replaced by a deficit. One person achieving success never means the automatic diminishment of the success of others, and belief to the contrary is the foundation of short-term thinking. And the converse is true as well. Failure at one juncture does not negate success achieved at a former juncture—in fact, the two should be able to coexist comfortably.

This is why I still believe that it is important to be comfortable with the idea that we can be part of the problem and part of the solution at the same time, a sentiment I expressed at that early Stockholm UN environmental conference. It is interesting (but I suppose not surprising) that I met many like-minded people at that conference, some of whom became my friends, such as David Rockefeller and Joseph Slater, whose Aspen Institute developed the core concepts for the Stockholm conference. My sense of direction and hope and my mission in life, particularly during difficult times, have always stemmed not from my work but from the people I encountered.

Certainly the period of time after my departure from Volvo was one of those difficult times. I may have been voted "Sweden's most admired man" nine times, but in the year after leaving Volvo no one approached me. I was very much alone in my hometown. And my wife and children also had to suffer the effects of what felt akin to a banishment. But at my core, I was unchanged. I remained an ardent humanist, one with the great fortune to be counted among the friends of other humanists such as Leonard Woodcock. And while I had closed the door on Volvo permanently, many doors had been opened to me during my time there, to exceptional people and places. And few of those people and places were more exceptional than Joseph Slater and the Aspen Institute.

CHAPTER FOUR

Humanism

Humanism: *in later uses after humanist (n)....after German Humanismus literary learning (1808), intellectual movement of the Renaissance (1847 or earlier), philosophy centring on the human (1848 or earlier)...French humanisme love of mankind (1765 in an apparently isolated attestation), philosophy centring on the human (1846, rare), intellectual movement of the Renaissance (1877).*

—Oxford English Dictionary

In 1978 I made my first visit to the Aspen Institute for Humanistic Studies at the invitation of Joseph E. Slater, the group's president. Both the institute and the man were to play a significant role in my life for some years.

I liked Joe Slater the moment we met, though like others I had some initial difficulty keeping up with him in conversation, as he often rushed through sentences in an attempt to keep up with his own thoughts or drifted off on a tangent. His penchant for operating at breakneck speed led one friend to describe him as "a three-stage rocket with all three stages firing simultaneously," and another to observe he was "a man born to have no rest himself, and to allow none to others." He was the kind of person who seemed to be good at almost everything, and that included his capacity for friendship. In the years that followed our introduction I was honored to count Joe Slater among my close friends.

Joseph Elliot Slater does not appear in many history texts. If a book-length biography or a documentary has ever been written about his life, I'm not aware of it. And yet both the scope and breadth of his work and his achievements are quite extraordinary, not just because of the varied disciplines they spanned, but because of the longevity of his time as a person of enormous influence in international politics. It is uncommon for an individual to be active and effective in the political world over the course of four or five decades. But Joseph Slater had an innate understanding not just of the work he did, but of the commitment involved in sticking around in the infinite lapses between the bursts of activity, knowing that the ebb and the flow were both crucial parts of the same process. He liked to repeat a story that the physicist Niels Bohr once told him about an exchange he'd had with Albert Einstein about productivity.

"When I asked him," Bohr told Slater, "Einstein said he only had two and three-quarters hours of productive life in his whole lifetime." Bohr then continued, "I know exactly what he meant! I had thirty-five minutes in 1911. I sat down transfixed in a Copenhagen street, sat on a bench…in thirty-five minutes, twenty years work came to me. And it took me twenty years to get back to those thirty-five minutes." Slater would add that those were twenty years of enormous work, and that staying with something until it's done (which is no mean feat when one is talking about the Copenhagen Interpretation) was one of the hardest parts of such work. The fascinating thing about Joe Slater was his capacity to do so much for so long. I think he had Einstein's two and three-quarters hours beat.

At nineteen, Slater joined the navy following the bombing of Pearl Harbor. He was commissioned as an ensign, and by the time of Germany's defeat in May of 1945, Slater was working with the Four Power Allied Control Council to oversee German compliance with the terms of unconditional surrender. His work in the de-Nazification of Germany (as the *New York Times* called it) was often grueling, and he counterbalanced the stress with music, offering his home as a venue for local chamber music performances, and befriending the composer, conductor, and Thomaskirche organist Gunther Ramin. He also taught himself German, believing it of paramount importance to be able to understand the political conversations of locals in order to do his job effectively. It was in Berlin that he also first met his future wife Annelore Kremser, a German-born Jewish American who had returned to the country of her birth to search for family who had gone missing in the Holocaust.

Slater's postwar CV continues to read like something dreamed up by Walter Mitty. As a member of the US State Department's policy planning staff, he worked to establish the United Nations, then served as executive secretary in the office of the US representative of NATO, and for the Organization for European Economic Cooperation. He left Europe in 1953 for Venezuela to become Standard Oil's economic chief at the Caracas headquarters of one of their subsidiaries, and later joined New York's Ford Foundation. In 1961 he became deputy assistant secretary of state for cultural and educational affairs under President John F. Kennedy, during which time he helped form the Peace Corps.

In the summer of 1967, Slater became acquainted with two burgeoning organizations: the Jonas Salk Institute for Biological

Studies in San Diego, and the Aspen Institute for Humanistic Studies as a scholar-in-residence. Both groups were seeking a new president, and perhaps it is not surprising that both asked Slater to consider taking the position. He accepted the Salk Institute's offer, but Aspen never gave up its efforts to hire him, and after serving for four years Slater stepped down from Salk to become president of the Aspen Institute. In *Genesis of the Salk Institute,* Suzanne Bourgeois writes about the future the Salk Institute might have known if Joseph Slater had remained its president, saying it "would be a different place today, perhaps with broader goals and deeper impact than a pure research institute." Instead, Slater's successor "killed the original spirit of Jonas' institute without providing a solid basis for its expansion."

I find that story to be very telling, because it was my personal experience at the Aspen Institute in the late 1970s that group's spirit and vitality was a direct result of the presence and guidance of Slater himself, and never the other way around. This is not necessarily unique to Aspen; I don't believe that any institution can indefinitely retain its vital core without the active interaction of a like-minded leader. In this way, institutes such as Aspen are like corporations; there must be constant work and renewal both in order to evolve the company and to maintain the integrity of core principles. Those renewal efforts don't occur automatically; they must be initiated and guided by an individual. And more often than not, this does not consistently happen over the course of the years. One reason I do not enjoy serving on organizational boards is that so many of them operate on automatic pilot, requiring nothing from a trustee beyond physical presence and the rote repetition of a single function. But soon after I arrived at the Aspen Institute for the first time, I realized that something rare and exciting was occurring. Things were happening. The pump, as they say, was primed. And Joe Slater was the one who'd primed it.

The programs in those days were small. In the first years I attended there were perhaps just forty or fifty participants. The intimacy and characteristically electric atmosphere at the Aspen Institute during the Slater years was in part due to the small scale, but also derived from the blend of people—politicians, top academics, scientists, and world-class musicians from all over the world—and of course a few people from the business world like me.

By the mid-seventies, the Aspen Institute was flourishing as the realization of Joe Slater's vision to create an authentic institute of humanistic studies. The institute had been around since 1949, the year industrialist Walter Paepcke conceived of an inaugural conference in Aspen to celebrate the bicentennial of the birth of Johann Wolfgang von Goethe. The keynote speech at the Goethe celebration was delivered by Albert Schweitzer, and his appearance at Aspen was to be the only visit he would ever make to the United States. The program and accompanying music festival were successful enough for Paepcke and his partners to conceive of something permanent at the Aspen site: a facility for continuing education that would concern itself not just with the humanities, but with human issues, and human solutions. As the idea took hold, Paepcke referred to his brainchild as a "High School of Humanities," but it was ultimately given the more suitable name of the Aspen Institute for Humanistic Studies.

The institute offered seasonal programs, executive seminars, and musical performances throughout the 1950s and 1960s, and they included some impressive speakers, among them Leonard Bernstein, Thurgood Marshall, and Robert Kennedy. When institute president William Stevenson began searching for a successor in 1967, his first choice was Joseph Slater, but he was not available. Stevenson was patient, and persistent. Two years later, with the offer of total freedom to design the Aspen programs as he saw fit, Slater accepted the job, and formulated his Five-Year Plan that would usher the Aspen Institute from modest organization to a world-class phenomenon. Joseph Slater had a profound intuition about the practical, real-life applications of humanism and the complex layers of knowledge and understanding that a leader must bring to bear. Whether working to solve the problems of a small group or a cluster of nations, the core issues "...just don't lend themselves to that sort of simple solution or easy pattern. There's a whole construct of...things and people and ideas, knowing about other civilizations, knowing a sense of history, knowing where values came from, which ones were discarded, which ones were kept. What commitment does a society or group have to the present, what vision, if any, of the future?" If you were unclear on even one of those things, he cautioned, you were in trouble.

Slater was an intellectual star, and the personal embodiment of humanistic qualities, a great lover of music and literature, exceedingly well versed in international politics, and someone with a genuine affinity for the working man. When he made his commitment to Aspen, he made it for the long haul. He believed that an effective leader had to have the patience to stay the course. And he identified a specific set of qualities necessary to lead, among them, "the ability to be committed, the lack of cynicism, a sense of humor, sense of fairness, a sense of openness, ...curiosity, a sense that an individual and certainly a group of individuals can make a difference...a sense of seeing the relationship between the individual and spiritual affairs on the one hand, and social constructs on the other."

In some ways, Aspen became a place molded from Slater's own experience in the world—a world comprised of intellectuals, diplomats, musicians, and political leaders—worlds he moved in with ease, confidence, and expertise. As a guest at the Aspen Institute you might lunch with a head of state, dine with a literary giant, and spend the evening listening to a virtuoso violinist playing Beethoven. When you were told, "There's someone over there who'd like to meet you," you were prepared to come face-to-face with anyone from an unknown artist to a political giant.

I had such an experience one night after participating in a panel discussion. At the end of the program, a heavyset man with thick, black-rimmed glasses walked over to me, and in a heavily accented baritone voice, said, "Young man, we do not know one another, but I think your contribution to that panel was exceptional, and very well presented. I would like to introduce myself."

"There is no need," was my reply, since to me (and most people) Henry Kissinger was instantly and unmistakably recognizable. We stood and talked for some time, and that conversation led to a friendship that has continued for four decades. I don't know that I expected to like Kissinger, but I did, or rather found that there were things about him that I liked very much. He is very bright, of course, and can speak intelligently on any number of subjects, displaying a wry sense of humor, which included the occasional self-deprecatory joke. He is an especially skilled historian, with the ability to zero in on the one true note amidst the cacophony. His longtime friend Dr. Fritz Kraemer explained it by saying, "The best way I can describe it is to say Henry Kissinger is musically attuned to history. This is not something you can learn, no matter how intelligent you are."

Kissinger is a reliably complicated person, and so of course there were things I did not like about him as well. I found he could be quite cruel in his judgments—even brutal—but I accepted that. It is and long has been part of his job and his persona, and the fact of it didn't surprise me.

Kissinger's relationship with the Aspen Institute was directly attributable to Joe Slater's presence as the head of the organization. From the outset of his tenure as president, Joe Slater was given free rein to design the blueprint for Aspen's programs and its core mission. The programs were focused in six categories: Communications and Society; Environment and the Quality of life; Education for a Changing Society; Science, Technology, and Humanism; Justice, Society, and the Individual; and International Affairs. In Sidney Hyman's *The Aspen Idea*, Slater's blueprint is described as sponsoring programs facilitating "thought into action" built on a foundation that would "concentrate on a critical number of areas, embracing interrelated and trans-societal issues, and seeking to illuminate from within the nature of the alternative choices they pose. In Slater's own words, "What the individual deplores...he deplores narrowly from a parochial perspective, and the world cannot afford that kind of narrowness any more. All the great issues of the day are not unique to this or that local community, or to the United States itself. They penetrate the frame of all societies."

The unique blend of intellectuals and politicians, right- and left-leaning, of leaders and followers somehow fostered precisely the "thought into action" atmosphere that Slater intended, quite probably because he was quietly at the center it all. He continued to be a real influence on certain leaders in the free world, often playing a key role in problem-solving. The extent to which Slater was seen and consulted as an influential force for his experience and international expertise, is evident in a February 6, 1980, "Eyes Only" memo to President Jimmy Carter from senior advisor Hedley Donovan, raising concerns about German Chancellor

Helmut Schmidt after his attendance at a closed group meeting in an Aspen Institute workshop held in Bonn. The memo reads, "Joe Slater, president of the Aspen Institute, has been involved with German affairs for 35 years and is thoroughly familiar with the rhythm of German insecurities no matter who is in power in Bonn—or Washington. He says what he was hearing last week was definitely above the 'normal' level of German anxiety and expressed with more than the 'normal' Schmidt acerbity." Detailing concerns stemming from American strategic doctrine and the Soviet nuclear threat, the memo concludes with Slater's analysis that the German leader was "increasingly worried about his domestic political situation" and "in need of major American hand-holding."

Slater's ability and willingness to play that under-the-radar problem-solving role had something of a contagious effect on his Aspen guests, and while there, each of us was primed to interact with other guests with the expectation of asking or being asked to do something, which could be anything from a modest collaboration to a significant undertaking. I've found no effective way to convey that other than to show from personal examples the kind of work that a meeting with the right person at the right time led me to. One of the more significant of such experiences came not long after my first visit to the institute.

I was taking part in a program session along with Henry Kissinger that included a discussion and a debate. Afterward, people took the opportunity to remain in the hall to talk to one another, as they often did. I stuck around to chat with them and saw a young man in a well-tailored suit was moving toward me in long strides, He had a neatly trimmed goatee and dark eyes that glittered with intelligence, and in spite of his youth he had the air of someone who was accustomed to being noticed.

He introduced himself as Prince Bandar bin Sultan Al Saud, son of the Saudi Arabian Prince Sultan bin Abdulaziz Al Saud.

"It is very nice to meet you," he said. "You spoke very well. I would love for you to come to Saudi Arabia." That, I admit, was not what I was expecting him to say.

"Why?" I asked.

He smiled and inclined his head slightly, saying, "Let us find a place to talk quietly."

We found a small cluster of chairs in a suitably private alcove and sat down. I waited for Prince Bandar to speak first.

"I've listened to you speak tonight," he said. "And I must say, I think you could help us. My father, Prince Sultan, is the minister of defense and he is in the inner circle in my country. He is a person of influence. I would like to have a discussion with you, and I would like you to meet with my father."

"Why?" I asked.

"I think we could develop Saudi Arabia, help it become more contemporary," he said. "What do you think?"

I had no intention of condensing my words into diplomatic platitudes. This was a place for direct and simple discourse, not pleasantries wrapped in a shiny bow. I had no doubt Prince Bandar knew that as well, and that it was one of the reasons he had sought me out.

"Well, I don't think it would be very difficult," I said, "because at the moment you are more or less living in the Stone Age."

"I think that's a bit harsh," he replied.

"Well, I think it's true."

He made a small agree-to-disagree gesture and leaned forward. "I want to modernize our country," he said. "That is the discussion I want to have with you, and that is the reason I would like to bring you to meet my father."

"Well, Prince Bandar," I told him, "if that is what you want to do, I would be very pleased to help you."

So our project began the Aspen way—with a discussion between two people who understood the value of direct discourse, and had no need for the trappings of formal diplomacy. Over the course of several talks it became clear to me that expecting a dictatorial regime (and its thousand princes) to make a smooth transition to democracy would be too drastic a step for Saudi Arabia. I knew both intuitively and by experience that this kind of rapid change in a dictatorial country would leave it prone to damaging aftereffects and, in all likelihood, only lead to a new dictatorship in the end. The pragmatic solution would be to devise a one-step-at-a-time scheme that might not move Saudi Arabia into the future by great leaps and bounds but would consist of step after prudent step in that same direction.

"I will come up with a plan, and you can see whether you like it," I told Prince Bandar, and he agreed. The proposal I created for him involved the creation of an assembly of perhaps 10,000 people, not from the royal family but educated people in the sciences, technology, in liberal arts—people chosen by virtue of their knowledge of the world outside Saudi Arabia, people who had studied democracies and other ways of ruling a country, and for this assembly to be the first step in according the Saudis some influence in their government. That would be a decent start, and not one prone to fomenting a revolution.

Prince Bandar seemed keen on this idea, and so I accepted his invitation to travel to Switzerland to meet his father, who owned a villa on Lake Geneva. Though I had gone to some trouble to prepare a paper outlining the idea I had presented to Prince Bandar, I hadn't been entirely certain my meeting with his father would come about. But here I was, in Prince Sultan's villa, momentarily at a loss for words as a servant offered me tea in a cup of pure gold. For a second or two I thought, *This is all too much.* No sooner than the thought was completed, Prince Sultan entered the room.

"My son is delighted to have gotten to know you, Mr. Gyllenhammar," he said. "Please, let us talk. Tell me about your idea."

My impression of Prince Sultan bin Abdulaziz was that he cut quite a figure, both physically and in the way in which he presented himself, as befitted the third most powerful man in the country. Unlike his son, Prince Sultan wore traditional dress: a white gown-like *thobe*, over which was draped a brown gold-trimmed robe, with his head covered with a long white *keffiyeh* headdress bound with a black cord. He was a large man who carried himself with a regal bearing (and indeed some years later would become the Crown Prince), but he was also capable of exuding warmth when he chose.

I described my hypothetical assembly of educated (but non-royal) Saudis.

"And why will this work?" he asked.

"If the people are presented with this assembly as something that the inner circle sanctions, and that the King himself has chosen," I said, "made up of people chosen by him, then they will feel safe in accepting the assembly, and they will accept its purpose is to give them a voice and an influence in the Saudi Arabian government. That could constitute the beginning of a democratic process that would spread throughout the country, making people more comfortable with being open minded. And it is important that this is designed to happen slowly, one step at a time."

"Why is this important?" he asked.

I explained how it made the difference between a making a decent start and risking a revolution. Any time change was pushed, and people expected to accept too much too soon, instability would follow. "This gradual change also acts as an encouragement to the rulers to be more outward looking, and to feel comfortable enough to be less defensive and protective and understand how much the world may be interested in this change."

"I see. Please continue," he said.

Our dialogue went on for several hours. I knew it was important that I not alarm him with my cautionary words about pushing too much change too quickly, but at the same time I needed to say enough so that my argument for gradual change could penetrate and be fully understood. He was very polite and seemed fairly impressed—not by me, but by what I had said. When I felt I had talked enough to convey my point, I brought my explanation to a close.

"This is very interesting," Prince Sultan said, and I believe that he meant it. "I will speak to the King. We will reflect on this, Mr. Gyllenhammar, and then we will get back to you."

I did not hear from Prince Sultan bin Abdulaziz again.

I was not overly surprised, though it was a little disappointing. I had done what Prince Bandar asked of me, and Prince Sultan had listened with every appearance of having an open mind. I don't think I could have made a better argument, and I don't think there would have come a better time. Prince Sultan heard me and understood me, but like so many others he capitulated to the overwhelming pressure to disappear back into the old ways, to cling to the ancient status quo. The Saudi people I encountered that year, those who were in the limbic place between past and future and willing, soon disappeared, and fear resumed its rule. When speaking of the Middle East, Henry Kissinger would often say "we went to the desert, but the only thing we saw of the Saudis were their footprints in the sand."

In the ensuing years, Prince Bandar would become the Saudi Arabian Ambassador to the US and bought a nice property in Colorado near the Aspen Institute, where he was a frequent guest. Thirty years later he was appointed director of the Saudi Intelligence Agency, and he became increasingly less friendly in his position toward the US. The young man of barely thirty whom I had met at Aspen disappeared gradually into the desert of those decades. If he left his own footprints in the sand, I know in which direction they ultimately went: back to the safety of the dictatorial past he had once sought to leave behind.

Regardless of the outcome, the Saudi Arabian project and my experience with Prince Bandar gave evidence of the kinds of things that could and did happen at the Aspen Institute frequently and was proof positive that Joe Slater's "thought into action" model was working very well indeed.

After my return from Geneva, I met with Joe and gave him a detailed account of what had transpired. He did not seem disappointed in the outcome either, because the fact that Prince Sultan had considered my words and my ideas was a triumph in and of itself. Not long afterward, he told me he had taken the initiative to take on a new project. This one, he told me, was fairly large in scale, and its implementation would be complicated, to say the least. But the potential gain was incalculable. And the time, Joe believed, was right. And even without my modest Geneva summit with Prince Sultan, Joe thought I might be just the person for this new project. I asked what the gist of it was. Fairly simple, he told me. A peace initiative of sorts.

"Where?"

"The Middle East. We want to send a delegation to help mediate between Egypt, Israel, Jordan, and Palestine."

That got my attention.

"Pehr, would you be interested in leading the delegation we're putting together to meet with Sadat and Begin?"

I shook my head.

"No," I replied. "I'm sorry, Joe. But I can't work with a delegation of people." Joe just sat there, his usual stream-of-consciousness chatter muted, as if he knew I had something to add. "But I'll tell you what I would do, Joe. I'll go to the Middle East and I'll talk peace with Sadat and Begin and anyone else who's interested, but on one condition. I go alone."

CHAPTER FIVE

Diplomacy

Diplomacy *(n): the science of formal intercourse between nations through authorized agents; the art of negotiating and drafting treaties;" more loosely, "transactions and management of international business in general," 1793, from French diplomatie, formed from diplomate "diplomat" (on model of aristocratie from aristocrate), from Modern Latin diplomaticus (1680s), from Latin diploma (genitive diplomatis) "official document conferring a privilege".*

–Oxford English Dictionary

I was waiting for Joe to respond to my suggestion that I go to the Middle East alone. My belief was that the way to get things done was with individuals face-to-face, not teams. Moreover, I knew Joe felt the same way. So, I was pleased when he said, "Okay, Pehr. No team. But you have to take somebody with you—even if it's just one person."

"Agreed," I replied.

So, in a quintessential Aspen moment, I had been asked and had accepted to undertake a project of great proportions—to examine firsthand the issues relative to the regional peace process. This would be accomplished primarily by my visiting three countries including Egypt, Israel, and Jordan and the territory of Palestine.

Aspen was really an extraordinary institution at this time. Slater had etched it firmly on the map and he was at the top of his capacity to make Aspen great. Aspen's board was prominent and diverse, made up of people who were having a real impact on the world outside of the United States. They were the people who decided to take a serious look at the Middle East and examine firsthand the issues relative to the regional peace process. They had discussions with each of the nations in question. In spite of the speed with which I accepted the offer, I was under no misconceptions as to the scope and complexity of the prevailing climate.

In the early 1970s, hostilities in the Middle East were creating political fault lines in all directions. There were continually deteriorating relations between Israel and its Palestinian neighbors, and tensions flared again when eleven members of the Israeli Olympic team in Munich were assassinated by an extremist Palestinian group. And in October of 1973 the Fourth Arab-Israeli War erupted. Despite rhetoric to the contrary, the nations of the so-called "first world" were not in a position, politically or otherwise, to firmly and fairly broker any sort of a peace in the region.

The nations, religions, and ethnicities of the Middle East were at an extended impasse, and no power outside the region had the objectivity, the knowledge, or the will to provide meaningful and effective guidance. It was a truly stunning moment, therefore, when Egyptian President Anwar Sadat announced he would visit Israel and address the Knesset with a call for peace. In the resulting address, Sadat offered Egypt's recognition of Israel as a nation, with the right to live within secure borders.

I was in London on November 19, 1977, the day that Sadat arrived in Jerusalem, the first and only Arab leader ever to take such action. I watched the news coverage on television. Sadat was smiling as he made his way down the plane's air-stairs. That image has remained with me to this day.

The Camp David Accord and the ensuing 1979 peace deal between Israel and Egypt was not the final chapter in the long-troubled region. Instead, it fueled the flames of discontent, angering both those who thought Sadat had given too much and those who thought Menachem Begin had settled for too little. Within the Aspen Institute, numerous meetings were held in which various viewpoints and priorities were discussed. In order for me to be an effective arbiter, I had to understand as completely as possible not just what each side wanted, but why. As Joe Slater repeatedly made clear, peace was not a mathematical equation to be solved by adding from one side and subtracting from another. Peace was not a function of borders or territory or firepower—it was a function of human beings.

Certainly, Palestinians needed their own country, but it was equally evident that the Israelis needed shared access to a small portion of the territory, and to safeguard themselves from pro-Palestine neighbors sworn to the destruction of Israel. There was a growing consensus during these meetings that the West Bank should be designated the buffer territory, and that Palestine be accorded co-rule with Jordan. The fact that we could even discuss hypothetical scenarios and reach a consensus shows how different the disinterested participants at Aspen approached problem-solving than partisan negotiators.

As Slater himself put it, "Peace is not merely the absence of war, as has been said so often, but peace means that there's flow of medical supplies and knowledge, that there's a flow of people, joint transportation, communication, food, agriculture, [and] water arrangements among nations; that there's sharing of knowledge and technology. Peace is a very positive notion of things that get done, that make sense, that are humane, and which are the fruits of the lack of physical military conflict."

In connection with the Aspen mission, I had been advised by Joe Slater to meet Britain's Foreign Secretary, Lord Carrington. I contacted his office and he must have been expecting my call, because he agreed to see me promptly. Lord Carrington, one of England's legendary foreign ministers, had a humor and charm that made him a very special man. As described on NATO's website, "Carrington was particularly refined, cultivated and personable. He knew the names of all his staff and treated them like family. Whether he and Lady Carrington were organizing an impromptu dinner with aristocrats and artists or a simple picnic with his staff, all were treated with the same respect and consideration." He showed great interest in my case and was very helpful in giving introductions to those he thought would be useful to meet.

Some years later I asked Lord Carrington to join the Volvo International Advisory Board, and we became lifelong friends. I used to visit him in Brussels after he became Secretary General of NATO in 1984. He always seemed pleased to see me. A large part of his duties entailed acting as a deterrent to Soviet aggression, but as it happened, during his tenure things were relatively quiet on the eastern front.

"Come back and visit again soon, Pehr," he would say. "Come as often as you like. Things are rather dull around here." At the end of his five-year term, he greeted his successor, Manfred Wörner, with some expert advice, telling him, "Now it is up to you to bore yourself for the next four years, Manfred."

My Aspen Institute-arranged meeting with Lord Carrington was entirely off-the-record. While underway, I kept notes that I destroyed after reporting back to Joe Slater, and only consulted with a few trusted experts, such as Henry Kissinger. As a strictly private sector endeavor, we were not beholden to any political constraints or blueprints. When meeting with a head of state, I could speak freely without the need to represent the interests of any one nation, and in turn that head of state could speak freely without concern that a casual observation or suggestion might later come back to haunt him.

In the context of an informal mission with an Aspen employee, we embarked on our Middle East venture. Our first stop was in Israel to meet with Teddy Kollek—Jerusalem's fascinating mayor—and with the opposition leader Shimon Peres. Of all the leaders I met during that trip, it was Teddy Kollek who made the deepest impression on me. He was a generous and open person with an encyclopedic knowledge of affairs, a natural sense of diplomacy, and a deeply ingrained desire to have Jews and Arabs living peacefully side by side in Jerusalem.

Solidly built, with a leading man's classical profile, Kollek was instantly recognizable and when he was out walking the streets of Jerusalem, people flocked to him. He took me for a walk at Golgotha and it was fascinating. On every street he was greeted with smiles and salutations. He stopped to chat with anyone who approached him. He was very popular with both the Palestinians and the Israelis. He talked to them and they talked to him—and they addressed him not as "Mayor" or "Mr. Kollek" but simply as Teddy.

By all accounts, and from my own observations, Teddy Kollek seemed to be almost universally loved. Born in Vienna, Austria, in 1911, he skirmished with Hitler youth, then immigrated to

British-controlled Mandatory Palestine with other pioneers. During the war, he negotiated for the transfer of thousands of young concentration camp prisoners to England and was instrumental in helping countless other Jews to flee Austria. Asked to run for mayor of Jerusalem in 1965 by Prime Minister David Ben-Gurion, Kollek reluctantly agreed and was elected mayor—a position he would hold for almost thirty years. Jews, Muslims, and Christians alike held him in high esteem, and he in turn was tireless in encouraging cooperative coexistence, saying, "Jerusalem's people must find peaceful ways to live together, other than by drawing a line in the sand." For all his devotion to the ancient city, and the enormous amount of work his job required, Kollek took the time to enjoy his life, always savoring a strong cup of coffee, a good meal, and a fragrant cigar.

To walk the streets of Jerusalem with Teddy Kollek was to see the city in all its ancient and diverse splendor. His pride was palpable as he gave me a walking tour of the Jerusalem Music Center which he cofounded with virtuoso violinist Isaac Stern. He was equally comfortable strolling through the Arab quarter as the Jewish quarter.

I was reluctant to end our visit, but I had to be in Jordan the next day. To go directly from Jerusalem to Jordan was forbidden. One had to travel to Jordan via Cyprus. As the crow flies, Amman is just over forty miles from Jerusalem, but the route entailed backtracking 250 miles to Cyprus, then making the 263-mile flight to Amman.

Teddy Kollek told me to come to his home on the eve of my departure, and while I was there he placed a midnight call on a secure line to clear the way for me to go straight to Amman from Jerusalem. It was absolutely unheard of to fly directly to Amman without going to Cyprus. But we did. Our small plane took off early in the morning. Kollek had secured a commitment that we would not be shot down. We made the journey without incident.

I spent one day in Jordan in discussion with King Hussein and his brother. They were keen to have peace in the Middle East. Peace between Egypt and Israel already having been made, Hussein and his brother were fed up with the hostilities. Jordan was not a strong nation. but there was no discussion about that.

From there, I met briefly with Yasser Arafat, though he was in fact the true enemy of both Israelis and Palestinians. Arafat received me but said almost nothing and was very noncommittal. He knew that I was Jewish. It was a dangerous mission under any circumstances, and very few people knew where I was or what I was doing. Having circumvented the diplomatic channels, I had virtually no resources or protection. I had no bodyguard. Anyone could have shot me and been done with it. Of course, I did not have to visit to Arafat personally. I could have handed the task off to my colleague. But I went myself.

Arafat obviously had problems. It was doubtful what influence he had over high-ranking Palestinians in the surrounding Arab states. Arafat seemed to be suffering from fatigue and was altogether a fairly unattractive person. He remained silent during my short talk. I read his silence as a tacit acceptance of peaceful discussions. I was relieved to have the exchange over with and left for Cairo with no desire to ever see the man again.

For all the advantages of flying below the formal diplomatic radar, there were drawbacks as well. Backdoor talks and quiet meetings are not usually delineated with a neat, printed itinerary. When we arrived in Cairo, the hotel staff did not seem to know who we were, and though it was my understanding that we were to meet with President Sadat in the morning, I had absolutely no indication of how that was to be accomplished. I knew the meeting was set for 10 a.m., but the equally crucial detail of the location had not yet been shared with me. I could only assume that word would reach me in time for the meeting to actually happen.

The morning began in a state of confusion, with the clerk at the hotel's reception desk quite firm in his insistence that no one had called or asked for me, until it emerged that a porter had been carrying around a paper with an incomprehensible squiggle that was in fact my own name. Having unraveled the first thread of this mystery, I located a car and driver waiting for us outside the hotel and arrived at the government building in good time.

At precisely 10 a.m., my colleague and I were ushered into the presidential office, reminiscent of a library with its dark wood-paneled walls and bookshelves, and portraits of distinguished-looking people placed around the room. Anwar Sadat was a handsome, elegant-looking man with a long, narrow face and regal profile, counterbalanced by the warmth of his expression and manner. In person, he conveyed a much stronger impression than in photographs.

Sadat seemed very comfortable conversing in English without a translator, and once pleasantries had been dispensed with, he talked about his view on what America's role should be in the Middle East moving forward. It was plainly evident that Sadat's interest in accomplishing a regional peace was profound. He had felt compelled to visit Israel and Jerusalem to propose a separate peace, he told me, because he truly believed the initiative could be the first step toward a time of harmony. I don't think a leader who lacked Sadat's passion and charisma could have made such headway with Israel. And for all that Sadat was a compelling person, it was nonetheless quite remarkable that the stubborn and staunchly conservative Prime Minister Begin had gone so far as to put pen to paper alongside Sadat in an agreement with Sadat that paved the way for long-term peace between the two nations.

In fact, it did not take long for Begin's resolve to evaporate; his rigidity promptly returned, in contrast with the steadily increasing flexibility of the opposition leader, Shimon Peres. Like Sadat and Teddy Kollek, Peres seemed to have a multilayered and pragmatic view of ways in which the troubled region could solve the problems that had plagued it for so long, but Begin was increasingly prone to paralysis. Nonetheless, our talk ended with a handshake and a resolve for peace.

After another round of conversations in the region, I was to visit President Sadat again. This time I would meet him at his summer palace outside Cairo, and the hour and location and all other relevant details of the meeting were confirmed ahead of time, so that I was more comfortable and confident. Outside of that officious wood-paneled office, he was less formal and more relaxed. We had a very good conversation. He philosophized about his meeting with Begin, and I gathered that he found the prime minister something of a bore. "You and I will work together," Begin had told Sadat, but the peace process had already begun to stall; the prime minister grew increasingly more stubborn and irresponsible. Even as he related this, Sadat stressed to me that he felt he had established a connection with Begin, and that their dialogue was ongoing.

Sadat spoke about his long-term vision of cooperative economic development with Israel. He saw Israeli and Egyptian strengths as complementary talents and raised the possibility of cultivating the oceans in concert with Egypt's vast field resources. Below the level of the Nile's paved dams, there are green beaches adjacent to the water where almost anything will grow, but beyond that immediate vicinity the soil is arid and dusty. Sadat told me that he envisioned many ways to leverage the whole of the Suez and Aqaba to bring growth to industry, agriculture, and tourism. When he repeated something he'd said to Begin, I could feel the potential and the possibilities conveyed with his words.

"I told him, Menachem, I give you sweet water from the Nile," Sadat said, "and you create a garden." But as powerful as those words were, they did not move the increasingly immovable Begin. Having taken that first courageous step, Begin seemed paralyzed at the prospect of taking another. I think that if Anwar Sadat, with all his integrity and equanimity, could not persuade Begin to persevere, no one in the world could have done it. With everything I had learned, both at Volvo and at the Aspen Institute, I can't see how President Sadat could have improved upon his efforts, nor could he have been more respectful and sensitive in his behavior toward the Israelis. Some years later, an Arabic friend of mine who was a judge told me that when Sadat made that historic speech to the Knesset in 1977, he had studied the poetic Arab, which he conveyed to the Israeli Parliament. This was a very long-standing courtesy and could only be appreciated by those who lived in the region and knew that choice. Obviously, it impressed the Knesset. But there are some challenges out of reach of both diplomatic and private efforts.

There was no hubris at work in Joe Slater's belief that he could better handle certain diplomatic efforts with his own network of people. As Slater described it, we were essentially saying: "We don't want to hear what's negotiable tomorrow, we don't want to hear about Geneva, we want to hear what is your wisdom that your viscera, as well as your intellect, tells you the situation requires."

Equally important was the distinction that while our private sector Middle East project was functioning independently of official government involvement, it was in no way excluding them altogether. Aspen's unprecedented network of world-class influential people ensured that the right doors opened at the right time, and that the officials who needed to know of our project were quietly apprised, over dinner or a round of golf, or as in the case of Alexander Haig, on the tennis court.

I had first met the soon-to-be Secretary of State after his recent installation as chief executive of United Tech, a company for which I served as a board member. Haig was invited by his old company to a dinner after the meeting. It was a Sunday, and we played tennis in the afternoon. I was looking forward to spending some time with him to discuss some of the conclusions reached by the Aspen Institute's Middle East conversations. He gave the initial impression of being somewhat interested, but after I summarized our findings, he did not really have any comments. Years later, Lord Carrington told me that Haig contacted him immediately following our conversation, asking for information about me. Lord Carrington smiled in amusement when he reported that Haig wanted to know if I was a British agent.

What was not at all amusing was Haig's evident disinterest in my reporting that Sadat, Begin, Peres, Kollek, Hussein, and even Arafat were all disposed to agree to a cessation of hostilities. As astonishing as it sounds for an incoming Secretary of State, the prospect of a fast track to a Middle East peace did not interest him. He was a pretty steely character, as well as being boring and arrogant. I didn't even try to dine with him. Disregarding all that could have been achieved, Haig's behavior can only be explained by the fact that the incoming Reagan administration wanted nothing to do with anything seeded on Carter's watch. All that remained was what Haig and Reagan could not erase from the record: Sadat had gone to Jerusalem to advocate for peace between Egypt and Israel, and the Camp David Accord had followed. Of what endured, I had little to do with any of it other than visiting Sadat in his summer palace. It was a significant disappointment. But it was not a surprise. In American politics, this is par for the course.

Slater understood far too well the lack of continuity from one US administration to the next. The incoming president wants his own people in and his predecessor's people out. There was no desire to benefit from the accumulated experience and insight of the old hands. Reagan certainly didn't want anything to do with Carter's people. Instead, he appointed men like Haig, who was not even very well read. Carter was a very good human being, but very inexperienced politically. It wasn't until he left politics that the depth of his goodness became evident to the public. In analyzing Carter's biggest weaknesses, Joe Slater summarized them by saying "Carter didn't reach out."

President Carter was apparently unwilling or unable to mobilize sufficient force when he weakened near the closing of his presidency to implement a plan which could lead to sustainable peace and recognized borders for the State of Israel. It was hoped that President Reagan would be careful during the opening of his presidential term and take several years to repair any damage suffered by US-Israeli accords. If he did, we then still know nothing of it.

Who would benefit from lack of peace in the Middle East? Had Haig been smart, he would have said, "Come, let's have a discussion. Explain to me what could be done." No one would have needed to know the genesis of the initiative. What did his single-minded thinking—his refusal to accept the work of his Democratic predecessors—gain for him? He could have taken credit for it. We wouldn't have cared. He could have earned a legacy as the Secretary of State who brought peace to the Middle East. Instead, what is he known for? For his other serious mistake of trying to take charge of the US government when President Reagan was shot.

The simple rule is always to find the best person or people in central fields and support them in the most flexible manner possible. Let them come together and do what they do. Avoid imposing artificial goals, boundaries, and schedules. Eliminate, as much as possible, the complications and bureaucratic entanglement of review committees. Don't be afraid to engage someone who is, or who might be, smarter than you. Give them the work they most want to do and let them do it.

These are the principles we applied in the Middle East—with great success, as far as the principle parties involved were concerned. It still seems almost miraculous that we were able to bring together Israel, Palestine, and Egypt into productive and fruitful dialogue that resulted in the very real outlines of what could have been a very real peace.

That our efforts were thwarted by what I can only regard as the shortsightedness of the US administration that rose to power at the climactic moment of our conversation did not and does not surprise me, but it did and does disappoint. The ideals that brought together the great discordant leaders of the Middle East were just that: ideals. But in the minds of pragmatic people of good will, people who know how to get things done, an ideal is the best of all possible tools. To see the work of artisans thrown aside by fools and forgotten is not a happy experience. But it is one from which much can be salvaged and learned.

Institutions come and go, as they must. Almost any successful institution, whether a government or a foundation, eventually outgrows itself. If an institution has become ossified or corrupt or otherwise useless, it should be scrapped and made anew. The United Nations, for instance, began beautifully but evolved into a huge bureaucracy with a semi-corrupt culture. If you abolished the present UN and began again to build a similar organization, would it not be just the same set of problems again? The answer is no! Not if the founding principles are strong and clear and the men and women charged with implementing them stay focused on the originating impulse.

Ideals without pragmatic implementation are toothless; pragmatism without idealism is empty at best and evil at worst. Ethos is a house you build, in which you set a table where people of good will and intelligence can sit together—as we sat with Sadat and Begin and Peres and Arafat—and change the world. The Aspen Institute I knew was such a house. It was an honor to be a guest there.

CHAPTER SIX

Industry

Industry *(n): late 15c., "cleverness, skill," from Old French industrie "activity; aptitude, experience" (14c.) or directly from Latin industria "diligence, activity, zeal," noun use of fem. of industrius "active, diligent," from early Latin indostruus "diligent," from indu "in, within".*

–Oxford English Dictionary

In the first years of the 1980s, Europe (along with the US and many other areas of the world) was sagging under the weight of economic stagnation. The 1970s had been a very difficult decade, plagued by a recession galvanized by the oil crisis in 1973. Unemployment was high, job growth was low, and Europe was suffering from what German economist Herbert Giersch called "eurosclerosis." Financially, the European Union was on the verge of collapsing. In my view, governments were going to continue making the same mistakes—looking to assuage the problem by propping up failing sectors of industry and agriculture. It was obvious that something must be done to spur growth and industry—and the way to do that was to look to industries that were not declining to address foundational changes that would have a ripple effect into other sectors. Put simply, infrastructure was the key.

I called on Wisse Dekker, who was then head of Philips in Holland—quite a big corporation in Europe—and whom I had met several times. I discussed my ideas with him, and soon we brought Fiat's Umberto Agnelli into the conversation. We envisioned a by-invitation-only club of sorts, very small in number, to be comprised of leading industrialists—people in charge of major industries that were especially influential not just in their own countries, but all over Europe. This would by no means be a lobbying organization, nor a vehicle for legislative reform. The focus of this group would be to influence the decision-makers ourselves in order to devise and plan the implementation of a major trans-European infrastructural renovation. We would do this by showing them a sketch of a proposed project, along with a financial plan showing how the private sector could participate and invest in terms of bonds, loans, and credits. By presenting only an overview, we would avoid resistance from the local construction, industrial, and environmental arenas by making it clear that it was not our intent to decide who built what, or to meddle in local affairs in any way. I decided to call this group the European Round Table of Industrialists.

ERT began as a club of seventeen members, among them Germany's Karl Beurle of Thyssen and Wolfgang Seelig of Siemens; Italy's Carlo De Benedetti of Olivetti and Umberto Agnelli of Fiat; England's Peter Baxendell of Shell; France's Olivier Lecerf of Lafarge Coppée; Holland's Wisse Dekker of Philips; and Switzerland's (German-born) Helmut Maucher of Nestlé.

Though it was my intention to have representatives from as many European countries as possible, there was a notable absence of Nordic members. In Sweden, Norway, and Finland, the companies were just too small (or state-owned) to be considered of the "major" caliber we were requiring. Accordingly, I organized a separate gathering with Nordic corporate leaders, so that they would not be completely left out.

In our first ERT meeting, I talked about the need for Europe to lift itself from the rust belt, and the importance of freedom of movement in Europe to maximize the potential for a healthy, unified market. The concept of a unified Europe had become paralyzed, and rather than moving forward with integration, we were now losing ground. The kind of changes that needed to take place to galvanize the unified market involved taking significant steps with very high up-front costs—in other words, steps that many politicians would find themselves unwilling or unable to take.

Our plans for major infrastructure development in Europe caused several of our colleagues' consternation. They were convinced that this plan was utterly unrealistic, and two of them jumped ship. The dropouts were both British—they had no real taste for the work and didn't believe in the vision. We ultimately lost five members to this concern, and considering their lack of vision and courage, I was not sorry to see them go.

With our new European Round Table of Industrialists members in place, I launched the idea of taking on infrastructure reform in earnest. We were not inventors—and the purpose was not to create new technology, but to take a look at what was already in place and make it more efficient. Our focus was to be on the modalities, systems, and methods, which would be examined with aggressive pragmatism. It took some time to convince some of the ERT members that this would increase the productivity for all of Europe as well as the industries who used the structures. We started to talk about road to rail—looking at areas in which the really difficult passages were obvious—a prime example being that between England and France. We began compiling sketches of proposed projects, and named the overall program Missing Links. Ultimately our first program focused on three projects: an England/France link, a Scandinavia/Germany link, and a trans-European high-speed train network. For each proposed structure, we provided outlines related to construction, cost/profitability, and financing. As reported in a 1985 article in the *New York Times*, "Rather than just complain, Europe's Business Roundtable decided to act. And so…it put forward its $60 billion plan, which aims at revitalizing trade, increasing growth and promoting industrial efficiency by opening up Europe's clogged frontiers. The project, known as Missing Links, foresees a new web of tunnels, bridges and high-speed train tracks that will enable goods and people to move around Europe much faster. By increasing the volume of traffic, the project could make frontier controls appear to be petty nuisances and could strengthen political pressure for their abolition. As Mr. Gyllenhammar puts it, 'Our links make frontiers irrelevant.'"

When the Missing Links report was completed, I planned to contact prime ministers and presidents around Europe to initiate personal discussions. In addition to our broad-strokes-only approach, I knew the paramount importance of circumventing the politics, but not the politicians themselves. The involvement and assistance of French Finance Minister Jacques Delors was invaluable. He was a driving force in politics and extremely helpful, as well as being a fantastic spirit, and ultimately, a good friend. Delors agreed that the approach to heads of state must always avoid issuing prescriptions to individual nation-states, instead making it clear that it was delegated to them to decide on specific programs and policies. Part of our role was to demonstrate that support of a major infrastructural project would be a profitable venture, not a liability for the state. I decided that I would not call or write heads of state, but rather would visit them in person—I believed that such face-to-face meetings were a key to getting things done.

Once communication was underway, initial response from governments was positive. Momentum gathered, and it was time to go public. I knew it was a big moment. As Michael Noller and Nicola Fielder wrote in the essay "Lobbying for a Europe of big business: the European Round Table of Industrialists": "In April 1983 the first Round Table meeting was held. This was the 'first time that European CEOs organized themselves to address European policy matters publicly.' At a press conference following the meeting, Gyllenhammar spoke of the meeting as a unique moment in European history and indicated there was a common feeling among the industrialists that something had to be done in Europe. Shortly afterwards at a second meeting, a memorandum to Commissioner Davignon was completed. It was entitled 'Foundations for the Future of European Industry' and spoke first and foremost of the need to promote a unified European market."

I received surprisingly little resistance from the heads of state with whom I met. We were, after all, talking about an enormous investment of both time and money. But I knew that both the Missing Links proposal and the argument I was making in support of it were compelling. I stressed that some of this investment could be financed by the private sector, through instruments such as EuroShare, which would attract private risk capital. As for the profit potential, the long-term returns of the Mont Blanc Tunnel provided solid evidence of success. The tunnel was completed in 1966. Over the next thirteen years the flow of traffic (and hence the generation of cash flow via the toll) grew by about 20 percent a year. By the fourteenth year, the net income generated exceeded the amount of the total project investment. The newly constructed Paris-Lyon railway line showed a similar pattern. The success of these projects was no flash in the pan—it was in essence a matter of logic. Both the Mont Blanc Tunnel and the Paris-Lyon railway line created a means of travel that was faster and easier than any previously available. Better routes attract more traffic, thereby offering a consistent and sustainable income—it was that simple.

To pitch the Anglo-French tunnel, I had already approached Jacques Delors. I explained what we were doing and told him I would like to have his acceptance and initiative to create it. He was enthusiastic about the tunnel and indicated that President Mitterrand was receptive as well. He also informed me that the president would be making an unofficial visit to Madame Thatcher in two weeks' time. So, I knew I needed to organize a meeting with Mitterrand, so that I could speak to him personally before he met with Thatcher. Though I would have a number of occasions to sit down with Mitterrand in the future, this would be my first meeting with him.

President Mitterrand usually ate dinner at the Elysée Palace or at his home, but he happened to have plans to dine with Jacques Attali two days before the Thatcher visit. Attali was then serving as presidential advisor and would go on to become the first head of the European Bank for Reconstruction and Development. I knew Attali as well, so I asked to go along to the dinner, which would be held at Attali's home, as it would clearly be a private visit, not an official one. I was not there to dine, so I sat at the table and talked to Mitterrand as he ate oyster after oyster—each one going down with a little slurp. I recapped what Jacques Delors and I had discussed and argued that an Anglo-French tunnel was a key element in European infrastructure. The specifics of the design were to accommodate road and rail, by way of a four-lane motorway and two-track rail line. Mitterrand was enthusiastic, and indicated he was in agreement that the proposed tunnel would benefit both France and England, as well as the greater EU. Of course, he could make no assurance that Prime Minister Thatcher would agree.

Ultimately, Mitterrand's meeting with Thatcher proved to be a breakthrough, though not without considerable resistance. In her competent and firm way, she said Britain couldn't afford the proposed four-lane motorway. Her response to Mitterrand was, "No, I will not support that—I won't spend a penny of state money on this. I can only agree to support a railway tunnel." This was a huge mistake on Thatcher's part. Had they agreed to the motorway tunnel, the toll revenue would have covered the investment within ten years. The technology of drilling two pipes under the English Channel did not require any sort of miracle—it was pretty straightforward. When Thatcher made the condition that it should only be a train tunnel, what she was really doing was limiting the project to just one or two drilling operations instead of four or five. She cheated herself and her constituents, because with rail only they would never recoup any investment in toll income, while the motorway could have paid for the whole thing, with private enterprise and contracts paying the costs of the tunnel. The economics had already been proven—these tunnels have a very high return annually including the repair works expansion and renewal they have to pay for. Thatcher ultimately fooled her own cabinet—had they taken the taxpayers' money they would have been paid back in less than two decades. To make only a train tunnel was in essence calling for bankruptcy on that project. But Thatcher remained immovable on that point.

Mitterrand, on the other hand, understood the practicality of my proposal, and had the courage to be willing to implement it. He had undergone an impressive transformation, having spent his first year in office acting as a socialist, and gradually becoming quite liberal in economic matters. I think he was a very good president. Some years later, Mitterrand gave me the *Ordre national de la Légion d'honneur* (Legion of Honor), established in 1802 by Napoleon Bonaparte. I got it from him in the *grand salle* of the embassy palace, where I was one of six or seven recipients. I got the highest order of any civilian, over GE head Jack Welch (to his displeasure), as Mitterrand found me to be the industrialist of top rank because I worked for Europe and not only for myself. I was deeply honored and touched by this.

The European Round Table of Industrialists reached a good level of momentum fairly easily with most of the government heads we approached. Because of the enormous investment involved, some of the Missing Links projects that were decided upon twenty or twenty-five years ago are still underway today—so it's all being realized but slowly. Such ventures must by nature go at a certain pace both for reasons of financing and manpower.

From the European Round Table's inception in 1983 through the early 1990s, we maintained this momentum—presenting proposals and getting political cooperation and agreement. There was an almost ten-year period when almost all that we created and proposed garnered support. However, there was a finite number of these large-scale infrastructural projects. With all of them in various stages of operation by the mid-90s, the ERT began to transmute—it was in essence the death of the original, small group of people who were agile, interested, and committed to these very significant projects. In my opinion, the major infrastructure projects were the real substance as well as the galvanizing force behind the ERT.

The smaller-scale initiatives, such as the theoretical proposals on education, did not engage the same kind of people in the same way. There was simply much less to do, and at the same time the size of the group was growing and showing unmistakable signs of changing from an innovative club into a bureaucracy.

It is typical of most organizations today that unless they have energy, a soul, and common policy, they all gradually die and disappear, expanding and then collapsing under the weight of their own bureaucracy. In the previously quoted *New York Times* article, the reporter compared ERT to an earlier American counterpart—the Business Roundtable, which had similar goals in the United States. The article states that, "While the general goals of the two organizations are the same, the groups differ in many ways. The European group is much smaller than the American model—around 20 members, compared with more than 200—and instead of limiting themselves to lobbying activities, the Europeans have put forward an ambitious, $60 billion plan for spurring economic growth.…Unless Europe's frontiers are stripped of bureaucratic red tape, the Roundtable fears, the Continent will never be able to develop enough world-scale companies and winning technologies."

That article identifies not just the key differences between ERT and the American Business Roundtable, but also demonstrates the factors that ultimately bogged down the efficacy of ERT—namely its size, and the propensity of a large organization (be it private or governmental) to become mired in red tape. When that red tape began to wend its way through the ERT itself, it was time for me to resign and move on.

All too often, organizations never have that energy or common vision to begin with. The Bilderberg Group is, to me, a prime example. Bilderberg is a secret discussion forum for elite political and business leaders. Its first chairman was Prince Bernard, who was married to Holland's Queen Juliana. He became embroiled in a corruption scandal involving the Lockheed company, and was further discovered to have been a member of the Nazi party. This was fairly scandalous; Holland, which was occupied by the Nazis during the war, found itself with a queen who had married a Nazi. As a result, he was forced to relinquish his leadership and connection to Bilderberg.

I was invited to be a member and vice chair of Bilderberg. At first, I was not uninterested. Bilderberg was well known—they invited heads of state and members of government of important countries and also some businesspeople. But when I looked more closely at it I knew the group was not for me. I saw it as little more than an elite talking club—and on top of that, its secrecy was something I simply couldn't stand. Politicians are public servants—it is inappropriate for them to participate in talks with other leaders that they were not permitted to share with the rest of the world. I was particularly loath to see representatives of the EU indulging in this kind of secrecy.

From its inception, the European Union had the potential to become a wellspring of risk-taking and diversity. It began with six core states (Belgium, France, Luxembourg, the Netherlands, Italy, and West Germany) in 1957 as the EU predecessor, the European Economic Community. The first six countries that formed it were very defensive, but also very optimistic, fueled by the prospects of opening up barriers to trade and travel. Between 1957 and 1981, only four additional nation-states were admitted as members. But by 1995 an additional five nations were added, and by 2004 another ten. Today, the EU counts twenty-eight member states, which will become twenty-seven when Britain exits.

But I would argue that the EU has managed to survive its growth spurt without developing an outsize bureaucracy. The EU often gets a lot of unjustified criticism in this regard. In reality, even today the EU and different councils employ amazingly few people vis-a-vis what they do. A medium-sized city anywhere in the Western world will be bigger in bureaucracy than the EU. What they have created is something that in today's world is totally unique—namely that you have freedom of movement (if you are an inhabitant of a member state you have a passport that is valid throughout the union). And the union is today (once Britain exits) twenty-seven nations. That is a record level of freedom of movement since before the First World War. If you look at Trump today with his wall and nationalism and closing the US to any movement together with any other nation in world, the EU is a fantastic example to the world of what you can do.

What the EU is doing right is staying true to the objective of having a Europe where you can move freely—a continent that is now being threatened by nationalists in the Czech Republic, Poland, Hungary; now Austria is also showing signs of becoming fascist again. Those nations have rulers today who are denying all the principles of the EU, and as such they are a risk to freedom of movement throughout the European Union. The other members are still standing fast. A leader such as Angela Merkel is a real democrat. She has a passion for freedom, is an extremely useful engine for the EU, and is a pillar of strength. I almost refuse emotionally to believe that Germany could go to the dark again. But for the first time Merkel has had to create a coalition, a sign of weakness. It is very important that her successor has her power and her thirst for freedom and freedom of movement. I still think that the EU is a fantastic example for the rest of the world in how you can encourage freedom of movement with identity documents valid in twenty-eight countries. That example is unique in the world unless you go back to nineteenth century.

Whatever its flaws, every member of the European Union has, free of charge, valuable goods and services. Americans, particularly in the Trump era, don't seem to understand that you can't protect yourself over time, and you can't stop a global economy that's already coming. America is drifting dangerously apart from the rest of the free world. Bombarded by lies and scandals and the utter contempt for the rule of law coming from the White House, the American public seems to have been stunned into a kind of stupor. They are on the one hand at the mercy of a single politician—as Republicans and the infamous Trump base continue to dig in their heels around their dangerously deluded president—the rules of humanity and common sense have been supplanted by the rules of politics, but even the rules of politics have now changed completely. The old laws of cause and effect no longer apply. Criminal allegations, sexual improprieties, public false statements—transgressions that were considered career-ending just a few years ago occur on a daily basis. The infrastructure of American morality has collapsed. It is a sobering and alarming sight to the rest of the world. But Europe soldiers on, and while Trump burns bridges and dynamites tunnels, the EU continues to build them, though it is doubtful they would ever have begun if we had not stepped in to influence the politicians.

Left to their own devices, politicians will invariably bungle tackling large-scale infrastructure by prioritizing their own self-interest. Historian T.P. Wiseman, writing about the need for new roads in the expanding Roman empire, detailed the infighting and factions that developed in the late republic and concluded that, "In the cutthroat political atmosphere of the late republic it seemed better to do without new roads than to give any one man such advantage in the struggle for political power." This kind of gridlock at the expense of the well-being of constituents will sound very familiar to anyone following American politics.

In 2001, Bastiaan van Apeldoorn contributed an essay called "The European Round Table of Industrialists: Still a Unique Player?" to the book *The Effectiveness of EU Business Associations*, in which he analyzed the growth and changing nature of the European Round Table in institutional terms. His conclusion is that ERT has undergone an institutional transformation that is directly linked to the growing influence of Europe's transnational businesses, and that the two are inextricably linked, as the growth of these multinational industries is a direct result of ERT's early programs.

As to its relevance and efficacy today, van Apeldoorn writes, "The ERT is still a unique player in EU politics in several respects but it is less unique than it used to be for two reasons. First, activities of ERT, and its role *vis-a-vis* Brussels policy-makers, over the years have become more institutionalized, and with that more like that of established organizations. Second, and even more important, ERT's impressive success has to an extent made it into a model for both established business associations and for new organizations. The phenomenon of the Round Table is in fact, I maintain, a manifestation of a larger trend in which the evolving landscape of European business representation has become increasingly dominated by large, and increasingly global, firms and their CEOs."

While this is an impressive testament to the long-term change ERT helped to galvanize, it is to be hoped that the EU does not find itself, like America, with the corporate cart placed firmly in front of the societal horse.

CHAPTER SEVEN

Dialogue

Dialogue: *Originally (in Old English) < classical Latin dialogus; discussion, dispute, literary composition in the form of a conversation < ancient Greek διάλογος conversation, dialogue < δια- dia- prefix1 + -λογος -logue comb. form, after διαλέγεσθαι to speak alternately, converse.*

—Oxford English Dictionary

In 1994, I had the great honor of being invited to the opening session of the newly democratically elected South African Parliament in Cape Town, just several weeks after the presidential inauguration of Nelson Mandela. My host in South Africa was a woman named Frene Ginwala, whom I had met while working with the United Nations Refugee Agency. Mandela had just appointed Ginwala to be Speaker of the National Assembly, the first woman ever to hold such an office. A South African woman of Indian descent, Frene Ginwala was a longtime member of the African National Congress, with a dazzling intellect and a patriot's commitment to social justice. As a University of London-educated lawyer and journalist, she used her knowledge of the law to write searing condemnations of the apartheid regime. Forced into exile after the 1960 Sharpeville massacre, she helped other ANC leaders—most notably Nelson Mandela—to escape via Tanzania.

Mandela was captured and arrested in 1962, and served twenty-seven years in prison on charges of treason before his 1990 release by President F.W. de Klerk. The lifting of the ANC ban allowed its exiled members—Frene Ginwala among them—to return to South Africa. After his election, he asked Ginwala to be his new parliament's Speaker. She had not wanted the top job—and had hoped merely to be a parliament member. But Mandela told her how much respect he had for the institution, and insisted she take the lead role of Speaker, explaining, "You must run parliament in a way that carries on what we have done in negotiations, where we have tried to bring all parties on board, we've tried to involve everybody so that we take the whole of South Africa into this new arrangement."

Ginwala of course accepted and held the post for ten years.

I can only surmise that I was invited to this historic parliamentary event because of my actions some eighteen years earlier—in 1976—when I pulled Volvo out of South Africa for the sole reason that I hated the apartheid regime, was alarmed at its growth, and did not feel that Volvo could justifiably do business with a country that had such a repressive governmental system. My actions in divesting Volvo were not without consequences. For our South African workers from the Durban plant it meant the loss of hard-to-come-by employment. For those who were not black South Africans, the ramifications included taking a financial loss, and for me personally, raising the ire of my colleagues and the Volvo shareholders.

We did not publicize our departure or make a lot of noise over it—we simply left quietly. But of course, the fact of our departure became very widely known. The prevailing opinion was that it was all for show—it was widely theorized that Volvo must have been sustaining prolonged losses from Durban, and in order to save face, I had leveraged the political situation to make it appear as if we were closing up shop as a political protest. The simple fact that the business world had such a reaction (since the possibility that this truly was a stance against apartheid was apparently inconceivable) was reason enough to justify both my decision and my feeling that it should be done without fanfare. Anyone who cared to read the financial news or ask for a copy of our annual report would be able to see that Volvo's South African venture had been a profitable one. As it happened, it was the divestment from South Africa that caused Volvo to sustain losses, not the other way around. The company and I were both punished, and it was made clear to me that I was seen merely as an executive showing off and throwing his weight around.

Attitudes changed greatly in the ensuing decade. By the mid-1980s there was a global movement to topple apartheid, in spite of US President Ronald Reagan's open support for the regime. By 1988 both GM and Ford had divested from South Africa (though Ford was back six years later). In 1976, however, the year of Volvo's divestment, the most intense and widespread apartheid debate was still years away. At that time there were approximately twenty Swedish companies with a presence in South Africa (others included ASEA, SKF, and Electrolux). My early anti-apartheid stance made me an outlier. But I would not have done things differently under any circumstances. With the hindsight of history, I imagine it would be my Swedish colleagues and stockholders who might choose to undo their opposition, if given the chance to go back in time.

Sweden was among the first European countries to begin actively supporting South Africa and was a regular financial supporter of the ANC by 1972. In the era of the socially idealistic and internationalistic Social Democrats, and party leader and Prime Minister Olof Palme, the anti-apartheid cause was embraced in Sweden sooner and more publicly than other countries. National support for a free South Africa was so extensive that just a month after his release from prison, Nelson Mandela's first international visit was to Sweden to address its parliament, saying, "...you have provided moral and political leadership, which has inspired many others throughout the world and sustained us in those dark days in prison, when it was impossible even to guess when the terrible night of racial tyranny would give way to a new dawn."

I am just one of numberless people who have deep admiration for Nelson Mandela, particularly as a humanist. I admire him not just for his strength and his boldness, but also for his tremendous warmth, patience, and humility. I respect not just his vision and fortitude in fighting for the freedom of all South Africans, but also the integrity and strength of courage he showed in remaining a deeply committed humanist after twenty-seven years of imprisonment. As Frene Ginwala described it, "It was almost a natural kind of leadership, because he believed it so sincerely."

By the time of his election, much of the world either openly esteemed Mandela or had the common sense to stifle their dissent. When my then wife Christina and I arrived in Cape Town in May of 1994, Mandela's inauguration had occurred just two weeks earlier. The event made not just national but global history—attended by forty-five heads of state (and viewed around the world by a reported one billion television viewers). As Christina and I walked around Cape Town on May 24, the atmosphere was electric, and the air of excitement was still palpable. It was a fantastic experience to be in South Africa at that time.

Crowds of onlookers and reporters gathered on Parliament Street and in the surrounding gardens as the ministers and their guests ascended the parliament building's wide stone steps to the main entrance behind six massive white columns. With all 400 parliament members in attendance as well as a number of visitors, the large and brightly lit chamber was packed. Frene Ginwala had told us, to my great surprise, that our seats were in the presidential box in the center of the semicircular seating gallery. We were seated with other guests of President Mandela, most of whom were members of his family. From the box, we had a bird's-eye view of the entire parliament. There sat Mandela and his first deputy president F.W. de Klerk, the former president who had accepted appointment as the new president's number two man. There also was the second deputy vice president, Thabo Mbeki, who would eventually go on to become the second president of South Africa after Mandela. Frene gave the official introduction of the new president, who then gave a stirring talk galvanizing the nation to dive into the hard work of "creating a people-centered society through the implementation of the vision contained in our reconstruction and development plan." To this day I'm not quite sure why Frene Ginwala arranged for us to be seated in Nelson Mandela's box. Whatever the reason, it was one of the greatest privileges of my life to be there, and I'm sure I shed more than a tear or two watching it unfold.

The world has certainly come a long way since 1976, when pulling a company out of South Africa was cause for a significant backlash. It is certainly to Olof Palme's credit that his opposition to apartheid was so far ahead of its time. It was a courageous and principled stance, and those were qualities I admired in Palme both as a leader and as a person. Palme was a demagogue in the best sense of the word, but at the same time he was a bit dangerous.

I first met Olof Palme in 1969. I was then only thirty-four years old, and had just become CEO of Skandia, which was the biggest insurance company in the Nordic area. At the time we first met, Palme was still the minister of education (he was elected prime minister later that year). I liked him immediately and remember that we sat down after being introduced and had a good conversation. He could be quite charming, he had a brilliant mind, and he was politically very engaged and interested. He was a close ally to the prime minister at the time, Tage Erlander, who was almost like a father to the nation in some respects. Palme was very left leaning and radical when it came to his political views. One thing that was quite clear was Palme was unreservedly against the Vietnam War. He thought that the United States had made a serious mistake, that they had committed war crimes, that it was scandalous that they stayed in Vietnam and killed so many tens of thousands of Vietnamese, and that it was the murder of a people. He did not spare his words in saying so publicly. I think his views at that time were basically correct, but in his rhetoric he could go too far. A single example is a 1972 radio speech in which he likened the US's behavior in Hanoi to the mass murder of Jews and others at the Treblinka concentration camp—a remark that resulted in the US expelling the Swedish ambassador and freezing its diplomatic relations with Sweden for the next year. There were those, however, who later came to appreciate Palme's consummate willingness to cut to the heart of any matter, including US Secretary of State Henry Kissinger, who once sent a telegram conveying his personal appreciation for Palme's "frank presentation of...issues... which we found most interesting and useful." Certainly Kissinger was of the school that there was rarely a good reason to pull a punch. He appreciated straight talk. Kissinger was quoted as saying there were only two Swedes he could talk to—Olof Palme and Pehr G. Gyllenhammar, a remark that amuses me, but that I feel no compunction to speculate upon.

After our first meeting, I continued to see Olof Palme periodically. I invited him to join me on an airplane flight over Sweden's west coast, which he accepted. The reason behind my invitation was that his administration had decided they would give a cooperative company a site on the west coast on which to build a refinery. As I was very environmentally minded, the thought of industrializing any part of this region of miles and miles of unspoiled coast of islands, rocky beaches, and subalpine birch forest was scandalous. As we flew over the pristine landscape, I shared with Palme my frank opinion that they should say no to setting up that refinery, because to do otherwise would be a crime against the environment.

Unfortunately, we had encountered several spots of bad weather, and the flight had been experiencing increasing turbulence. Palme's complexion had gone from white to a peculiar shade of green. He unfortunately grew quite airsick, and was barely able to focus on what I was saying, or the beautiful landscape below us that was meant to be hammering home my point. With the tour completed, the plane turned back toward the airport. Once on the ground, Palme quickly recovered. But it was not a successful tour.

In spite of this, Palme agreed to join me on another trip over the north of Sweden—because he liked the idea of an overflight. This time, we had one or two politicians joining us in the aircraft. Once again, my motive was to argue against industrialization—this time in the north, where the boreal forests were already suffering the effects of unsustainable logging practices. Once again, I was arguing against the prevailing Social Democrat position, but my blunt words did not damage our relationship. On the contrary, they seemed to reinforce it. However, there came a time when I found it necessary to come at him more forcefully, when, around 1976, he wanted to socialize part of Sweden's economy through a program called wage-earner funds. Put simply, Palme wanted to require every company in Sweden to set aside a portion of their profits as a reserve fund in the form of shares for blue-collar workers, comprised of a combination of metal workers and white-collar staff. In effect, this would act as a gradual transfer of ownership of the company to the workers. This was something approaching a real socialist twist for our liberal and open Swedish economy. I strongly and publicly expressed my feelings that this socialization of the Swedish economy was unacceptable and very poorly thought through. At that time I said goodbye to Olof Palme, and he said goodbye to me.

This proved to be a complete break between the two of us. There was supposed to be a referendum on the issue, but nothing came of it—and the wage-earner fund that eventually was enacted was so different than the original proposal it was confusing to even refer to it by the same name. Palme and the Social Democrats suffered an electoral defeat that same year, but in the 1982 election he recaptured his position as prime minister. Our relationship never recovered from our difference on the point of the original wage-earner funds program, in spite of my view being borne out over time. After that I had practically no relationship with him at all. Things became fairly vindictive, as Palme simply couldn't tolerate me after this public attack on him, a position which I can understand. I only experienced something approaching a reconciliation with him following his assassination in 1986.

Like most people, I was quite shocked by Palme's death. The idea that he had been murdered still felt surreal when I received an official invitation from the Social Democrats to be a guest at Palme's funeral service, which was held in the enormous main hall of the Stockholm City Hall building. On the grand staircase at one end of the hall sat the white coffin underneath a mound of red roses, the symbol of the Social Democratic party. Security was extremely tight; there was a fairly large group in attendance and representatives of 145 countries. I was seated in the first row of people who were not party members, and I was moved and honored that they would remember me and extend that invitation, especially after our differences. After the service, the funeral procession traveled over the streets to the graveyard at nearby Adolf Fredrik Church. Over 100,000 people lined the streets to pay their respects.

The emotional climate throughout the city was a kind of collective shock and disbelief. It was different than the outpouring of grief that gripped US citizens after the assassination of President Kennedy. But it was a drastic loss when coupled with trauma from the violence that had caused it. Many Swedes felt such things just didn't happen here—until 1986, they hadn't. As unthinkable as it seems today, Palme and his wife had no bodyguards or security when the assassin intercepted them as they walked to their Stockholm flat after seeing a movie. That gives a sense of how unexpected the attack was. And in fact, no Swedish leader had been murdered since the late eighteenth century when King Gustav III was killed by an assassin's bullet. It was a true and honest mourning by the Swedish people, and it was reverent to him.

Ingvar Carlsson was unanimously nominated to succeed Palme. Carlsson was of the older era Social Democrats and had the kind of traditional solidity that was the hallmark of the party during the long period of supremacy that had seen it remain undefeated between the end of World War II and Palme's 1976 electoral loss. It was the kind of reasonable, moderate leadership that I think the party and the country needed at that time. As with many successful leaders, Carlsson's success was intertwined with both the national character and the national history of Sweden in that moment. No country stays the same from decade to decade—a successful leader must be defined by the needs and constraints of the nation as they arise. Someone like Carlsson could never have been elected in a dissimilar region of the world, such as parts of southeast Asia where the workforce is becoming more and more expensive. Singapore is a perfect example.

I first visited Singapore in 1968, three years after the country achieved sovereign independence. It was a time when the country was beginning to discover the correlation between a superior work product and competitiveness. Prime Minister Lee Kuan Yew had, as described in his New York Times obituary, "transformed the tiny outpost of Singapore into one of Asia's wealthiest and least corrupt countries as its founding father and first prime minister."

An American friend in Singapore had invited me to play tennis on a court he knew of near the Istana presidential palace and gardens. It was a typically warm and humid Singapore day, so the game was fairly exerting. I wasn't a great player, but that day my partner was really playing a lousy game. At some point I became aware of a man wearing a white shirt and pants watching us from the sidelines. We played a few more points, and the man was still there, so I walked over to him.

"Wow, you're playing here," he said. He was tall and slim, with a youthful face and a thick shock of black hair swept back from his broad forehead. "It's not too hot?"

I said something to the effect that it wasn't, and at more or less the same time I realized I was addressing Prime Minister Lee Kuan Yew, meaning my American friend's court was not near the palace grounds but on the grounds.

He looked somewhat impressed at my dismissal of the heat and asked me to introduce myself.

"I'm Pehr Gyllenhammar," I told him. "I'm visiting from Sweden. I'm chief executive of Volvo."

Prime Minister Lee nodded slightly, as if approving my answer.

"You should come and visit me one day," he said.

"I'd like to very much," I replied.

He turned to go, calling over his shoulder, "Contact my chief of staff!"

I turned back toward the court to find my American partner, who'd come up behind me, his face falling as he realized the departing prime minister was not going to ask him the same questions. I shrugged wordlessly and went back to the game.

As soon as I had the opportunity, I did call his chief of staff with my contact information. On my next visit to Singapore, I was invited to have lunch with Lee Kuan Yew in the guest office of the place. It was just the two of us, sharing a simple meal of rice, meat, and steamed vegetables—his penchant for healthy meals was well known even then. I was finding it difficult to relax, however, as there were two armed soldiers standing quite close behind my chair.

"Mr. Prime Minister," I began politely. "Is it necessary to have these people here?"

He looked up and smiled, saying, "You're the first person who's ever said anything like that."

"Well," I said. "I'm just a bit concerned. You never know what they will do, and you never know what I will do—that's why you have them, I suppose."

He laughed, and addressed the guards in Cantonese, telling them to leave, which they did. I thanked him. And after that we were alone, dining and talking in complete privacy. I asked some questions about Singapore, and we talked some about what I was doing (though I was much more interested in what he had to say). We eventually got into a discussion that was quite fascinating, about politics, about the state of things in Singapore, and about whether Singapore was a real democracy—which I claimed it was not. He tried to explain it to me, saying when he became prime minister, Singapore was a very chaotic place and not very well run. It had been necessary to create order and change the constitution, which was a fairly complicated business. And he was doing all that, he said, but in the meantime, he still had to rule.

Later, he introduced me to a few of his cabinet ministers. Some of them were Chinese, some Indian, some other minorities—representative of the mixed population in Singapore at that time. It was quite a skillful group. They were obviously extremely well educated and knew a fair bit about the world, which is necessary when you are in a very small island state threatened from everywhere, from the Chinese, from the Malaysians, from all sorts of places. It was imperative to create a very smart administration, and an excellent educational system—and Lee Kuan Yew was absolutely devoted to Singapore's educational system. He told me, "We will never survive unless we are on top of things and unless we have an education system that is one of the best in the world." Singapore had a military academy of course, which was important for them, but they also had a university system that was very close to world class and eventually became world class. I found all of this fascinating.

After that lunch he said, "Well, what could Volvo do for Singapore?"

"I'm not sure what we could do, if anything," I replied, "but perhaps we could have an assembly shop in Singapore."

His response was, "Mr. Gyllenhammar, don't even think about it. I want much more advanced industrial efforts in Singapore. Assembling vehicles that are already made and disassembled before they come here just to be reassembled again, no, I wouldn't think of that."

I thought that was very smart. And he was right, of course. You don't disassemble something just to assemble it again. It was an absolutely rational opinion, so I said fine, I understand.

All in all, it was a very good discussion. Lee was firm and open, and he was smart. That lunch started a friendship that continued to grow over the years. From then on, whenever I was traveling to Singapore I notified him, and we would meet in person. I really grew quite fond of him. We continued our dialogue and exchanged views by letter as well.

He was very consistent in defending his curtailing of civil liberties and free speech, making an argument that only a head of state could make. Lee Kuan Yew was definitely not a fascist. He strongly believed that it would be very difficult to create discipline in a state whose very survival was constantly under threat.

"Therefore, I need to be fairly strict with the people and not give them too much freedom of expression," he said. And he not only defended that belief, he defended it extremely well. He was quite sincere in his views. I didn't like some of them, and I continued to criticize them. And I didn't share his view on civil rights, which he knew. But given the circumstances, I accepted it.

This was a time in my life, in my early years at Volvo, when I seemed constantly to be meeting very remarkable people. Kay Graham was another, and she is someone I still consider a hero. I was invited to join her and her team for a lunch at Newsweek in New York shortly after I began at Volvo. She was a very impressive woman even then, before she took over the *Washington Post*. She was modest and soft-spoken, but at the same time sharp and brilliant. She had observed me and my position as a very young man becoming CEO of one of the largest industries in northern Europe. She had questions for me, which she asked directly, but never in the manner of a cross-examination. She did some probing but was elegant about it—in interviews as in all aspects of her life that I could see, Kay Graham had distinction, style, and taste.

We had a mutual esteem for one another, and in time we became good friends. I was aware of what she went through when her husband died and she took over for him, becoming editor in chief and publisher of the *Washington Post*. To say it was a major career move is a gross understatement. And I was not at all surprised that she handled it brilliantly. She emerged into the leadership role subtly, with a quiet and discreet authority, but there was no doubt she was in charge.

After that first meeting, I saw her several times when she came to London, and in other contexts as well. So, from the very beginning, I was a true admirer of Kay Graham. When Watergate surfaced, she rose to the challenge in a way that was simply awe-inspiring. She had the immutable faith, courage, and journalistic principles necessary to take on this task—and furthermore she had absolute trust that her reporters, Bernstein and Woodward, were making a fair assessment of what was going on, and with the likelihood of the president's involvement. She was heavily criticized throughout much of the process, but she stood strong, always absolutely insistent that her reporters were not only honest but fair, with a very good sense of where the truth was.

Without her unstinting support, Bernstein and Woodward could not have maintained their investigation, because the legal and political forces being brought to bear against them was massive. Nixon was a powerful president and had enormous influence in Washington and beyond, and he declared a vendetta against the *Post*, forbidding his press secretary to let any member of the paper into the White House for any reason. In that sense she had enormous courage to support them. And of course, history bore her out. Nixon was a corrupt, dishonest, and vindictive leader unfit to be president, and the work of journalists was crucial in bringing about his well-deserved demise.

At the time of this writing, it is almost inconceivable that the US has a sitting president who by comparison makes Nixon look almost respectable. They share negative qualities—vindictiveness, abuse of presidential power, gross distrustfulness of the press, a tendency to nurse a grudge, chronic dishonesty. But Nixon had positive attributes that Trump does not share. He was decisive, strategic, and highly intelligent. Trump is notoriously indecisive, chaotic, and without question the most poorly educated and unintelligent president ever to sit in the Oval Office. His vendetta against the press has been compared to Nixon's. In an article in the *Florida Times-Union* about Trump's threat to rescind broadcast licenses from any news station providing presidential coverage that he didn't like, the reporter noted Graham's recollection of similar threats, writing: "Graham said former Attorney General Richard Kleindienst contacted the Post in 1971 'threatening us with a campaign against the press and with criminal prosecution if we did not return the Pentagon papers after the Supreme Court decision allowing their publication.'"

Rarely has the world, and the US in particular, had such a need for strong and courageous leaders in politics, media, and business. Nelson Mandela, Frene Ginwalla, Lee Kuan Yew, and Kay Graham were all very different people with several key qualities in common: they were all intelligent, practical, and profoundly ethical people who could communicate effectively, who had an intuitive sense of leadership, and who had world-class levels of power. Each of them in their own way rocked their nation's foundations a little, and each one of them left the world a better place than they had found it. The link between leadership and journalism is complex and interconnected. Ethical leaders cannot endure without ethical journalists.

It was especially fitting, then, that after her tenure as Speaker, Frene Ginwalla became a trustee of the Reuters Founders Share Company in 2004. Few people know better than she the value of integrity, the power of communication, and the crucial importance of direct and active dialogue. When asked in 2008 to describe the legacy of Nelson Mandela, she replied, "That, I think, is the real legacy of his—that notion of dialogue. The right starting point is to listen and to try and get an understanding of the perspective of the person with whom you are engaging. What that brings about is a respect for the other person. You then don't start using labels like 'racist' and 'opportunist,' because you are trying to go behind those labels and see why that person is doing or seeing something in a particular manner. He respects the perspective of other people and he's tried to inculcate it in those who worked with him in the ANC, not always with success. I think that's a legacy that transcends any particular situation or country. So dialogue has to happen not to reach a solution but first to understand the problem and the perspective of the parties who are engaging. Only then do you reach a solution and bring reconciliation."

Given what she and Mandela endured and accomplished, it is a fairly simple assessment. The mastery of dialogue does not require an advanced degree, or a powerful network, or wealth. It is something almost anyone can cultivate. So why does the number of exceptional leaders seem to dwindle with each passing year? Why is courage in such short supply?

There is a widely published photograph taken by helicopter in South Africa on April 27, 1994. Against a backdrop of grass and red dirt roads, a serpentine line of people looped back and forth and around itself, containing hundreds if not thousands of human beings. The people were waiting in lines that extended several kilometers to vote in South Africa's first democratic general election. The results of that election are proof positive that even a fifty-year-old oppressive regime could be beaten back. And as history demonstrates, sometimes the unlikeliest and most sweeping change for good can be brought about by the actions of just a few, or even one bold and right-minded person.

CHAPTER EIGHT

Alliance

Alliance *(n): c.1300, "bond of marriage" (between ruling houses or noble families), from Old French aliance (12c., Modern French alliance) "alliance, bond; marriage, union," from aliier (Modern French allier) "combine, unite".*

–Oxford English Dictionary

The last years of the 1970s brought difficult economic times, with Europe struggling through recession. I was looking for innovative ways to protect Volvo and reduce its vulnerability. As a fairly adventurous and forward-looking person, my attention was drawn to the neighboring country of Norway, and more specifically to the offshore oil deposits on the continental shelf.

The oil and gas industry was relatively new to Norway. It was not until 1959, when a significant gas field was discovered in the Netherlands, just miles from the coast, that the possibility of other gas or oil fields in the North Sea was seriously considered.

Phillips Petroleum was one of the companies that applied for and received a license to search for oil fields. Years passed with no major discovery, but in 1969 Phillips found a massive oil and gas deposit in Norway's North Sea region that became known as Ekofisk. Norway was suddenly a player in the oil industry, and in 1972 Norway's state-owned Statoil was founded. It was highly likely that other deposits of oil and gas would be found. But as an industrial base, Norway remained weak.

In late 1977, I approached Norway's prime minister, Odvar Nordli, saying, "You have massive oil finds off your coast, so it is very likely more will be found. But your industrial growth is too narrow, and it has to expand beyond the energy and fishing sectors. I want to propose an alliance between Volvo in Sweden and you here in Norway that will also help you build and expand industry, particularly into engineering."

Nordli was fascinated by this idea and invited me to a series of private meetings in his home in Oslo, where we were joined by Bjartmer Gjerde, recently appointed Norway's first minister of petroleum and energy. The alliance I proposed was a quid pro quo in which Volvo would establish manufacturing plants in parts of Norway, giving Norway Swedish lumber and approximately 40 percent of Volvo's share capital, and in return Statoil would give Volvo oil concessions on the continental shelf.

Both in the private meetings and after broaching the idea with their parliament, Norway was very enthusiastic about the potentials of a Norway-Volvo alliance. I also had the preliminary support of the Swedish prime minister and the Volvo board. This was an unprecedented opportunity to create a new page in the history of Swedish business and industry, to have a company (as opposed to a nation-state) open the door to cooperation with Norway in a completely new and different way.

The Swedish public had admiration for the sheer audacity of the project—I was then still very popular as an individual in Sweden, somewhere in the midst of my nine years as the country's most admired person. The people were used to my adventurous nature and trusted me. But there was a growing opposition to the deal from Swedish big business and leading industrialists, because most could only focus on the fact that Volvo would bypass them and become too big as a result of the Norwegian project. The argument against the alliance began to play out in the press—critics claiming it was too risky, that there was likely no more oil to be had from their territory, in spite of the fact that Norway's oil fields were now among the richest on the continental shelf.

The story managed to hit the newspapers almost every day for months, and we held an extra shareholders meeting to address the deal. There was enormous speculation in the press from moment the Norway alliance was announced. The most common spin on the story was that the resistance stemmed largely from the Sveriges Aktiesparares Riksforbund, an independent association of Swedish shareholders, and that the increasingly organized campaign to discredit the alliance had been orchestrated by the Aktiesparares' chairman, Hakan Gergils.

I found it very naive of the Swedish press to believe and perpetrate this story, when it was clear to me that the stockholder association was little more than a puppet organization whose strings were being pulled by a powerful family dynasty of industrialists. I would have had more respect for the Wallenberg clan if they had been open and straightforward about their move against the Volvo-Norway alliance. As it was, it took the form of backroom talks to sabotage the deal, using someone else to act as a go-between to reverse the course. I felt then and still feel today that was a pretty dirty maneuver.

The Wallenbergs had dominated Swedish industry for decades, but they also represented the establishment, as I resolutely did not. The Norway deal was a significant departure from the norm, and with establishment resistance to the mere suggestion of anything Swedish being ceded to Norwegians, many shareholders could be and were persuaded to vote against the venture.

The meeting of Volvo directors to ratify the deal was scheduled for the end of January of 1979. I wanted the vote to pass by a qualified majority—meaning more than 67 percent rather than just over 50 percent. We held a proxy vote count a week before the scheduled official vote. The numbers fell short. We had more than 50 percent in support, but were about 7 percent short of a qualified majority. It was over, and the shareholders meeting was quietly canceled.

I had lost, and the opportunity was gone. It would not come around a second time. We had been in a unique moment in which many things aligned—with the leaders of both countries ready and willing to work together, and in a time before the oil money began to pour into Norway as it did later. The time for the alliance was now or never, and the necessary vote had fallen short.

We had, in essence, lost Norway. Of course, Sweden officially lost Norway in 1905 (which in retrospect was for the best) but we lost it again as a cooperative partner in that January day of 1979. At that time, it was Volvo—not Sweden—that I was fighting for. But nonetheless, I thought the Norway deal was a good way of helping Sweden expand in Norway when they had more or less given up. It was something that would have benefited so many, in so many ways. I felt very disappointed in my country, and it brought up some of those latent feelings of unease that I'd first experienced as a child during the war.

Some months later, I was surprised to receive an invitation from the head of the Wallenberg family, Marcus Wallenberg, asking me to an annual dinner being held at the end of summer. I RSVP'd that I would be unable to attend. Not long thereafter, Wallenberg called me. He told me he had invited about seventy-five Swedish executives to the dinner. "Only two of them declined," he said. "The first one asked my permission to miss the dinner. The second one is you." I politely repeated that I would not be accepting the invitation, but privately thought it was something of a victory that Wallenberg felt it necessary to call and personally inform me that I was the only one to unilaterally decline.

At the time, I had no clear idea of why Marcus Wallenberg would suddenly reach out to me. We knew one another, of course. Sweden is a small country, he was an industrial powerhouse, and I headed the nation's greatest automotive company, therefore we often moved in the same circles. And in the past, I'd had direct encounters with the family as well. The first was quite early on, when I was thirty years old and working at Skandia. I received a phone call from the then head of the family, Jacob Wallenberg, chairman of Sweden's oldest stock firm, Stora Kopparberg.

I can remember his voice over the phone, saying, "Is this Mr. Gyllenhammar?"

I said that it was, though I did wonder if perhaps he was looking for my father. I had only recently started at Skandia, and I was a bit surprised that someone so many levels over me would be calling.

"I would like to ask you to be auditor at Stora Kopparberg," he said.

The invitation was as completely unexpected as the call itself.

I told him yes, I would, even though I wasn't quite sure what an auditor did. I just told myself, *My God, I'd better take this chance.*

The SK auditing group had recently lost an auditor (who had either retired or died). And the head of the auditors was an amateur—a layman, and perhaps not surprisingly was himself a distant relative of Jacob Wallenberg. So I became the number three auditor, which left the other employees quite surprised, to say the least. Wallenberg, at any rate, made it clear that I was to be welcomed.

This was really something for me, as even back then in 1965, the Wallenbergs were the most powerful family in Sweden with enormous wealth and a vast corporate portfolio—some of the companies they owned included Electrolux, Ericsson, SKF, Atlas Copco, and Saab AB. In some ways, they could be compared to the American Rockefellers in terms of their wealth, influence, and top-dog position in society. They donated money to many institutions around Sweden, with the result that the Wallenberg name appeared on countless buildings.

I became quite close to Jacob Wallenberg while acting as auditor. After a few years, Jacob had some kind of break with his brother Marcus and the rest of the family, and he simply left, both the business and the family.

So I was no stranger to the family, and in fact, just before I pushed forward with my Norway alliance idea of 1978-1979, I explored another avenue for Volvo, which was the idea that Volvo merge with Saab-Scania. The Wallenberg-owned Saab was Sweden's other automotive company. Saab had two divisions: one was military aircraft, and the other was cars. Saab provided vehicles to the Swedish defense industry and were essentially subsidized by the aviation business. After forty years of existence, Saab had seen just two years of profit. Volvo, on the other hand, had enormous staying power—and even during that recession we were more or less profitable each year.

I proposed a merger with Marcus Wallenberg, and he said he was interested in discussing it in detail. Given his support for the idea, I said we should push ahead. A new statute ratified in 1976—"Co-Determination in the Workplace"—directed that worker representatives had to be apprised of any proposed change to the company, afforded the opportunity to bargain for their own terms, and must then either approve or reject the proposed change. I think Wallenberg was too conservative to get that the requirement was not just the law but very real in practice.

While we were negotiating about details of the merger, I began to hear things to the effect that the managing director was unhappy with the proposed fusion of the two companies. While the corporate details had now been hammered out and agreed on, the workers were nowhere near approving the deal. We were hamstrung. Wallenberg didn't understand why things were mired in a delay. I told him he was legally constrained from formally accepting the terms until the workers approved. That certainly wasn't going to happen until the managing director got the workers on board. Wallenberg somehow seemed to believe that if he told his management a project was a good one, they would automatically provide unilateral support.

The whole process went back and forth, becoming increasingly drawn out. The Saab managing director's official line to his boss was that he was making headway in the worker negotiations. Meanwhile, it had been leaked that the managing director was not only not working to secure an agreement from the workers, he was defying Wallenberg and refusing to solicit his employees' support. I suppose there was something he wanted to throw into the mix for himself, but as the negotiating process dragged on, I began to lose not just my patience but my confidence in the entire venture. I called Wallenberg.

"Your chief executive is meeting with workers and telling them he objects to this entire plan," I told him.

"That's impossible," Wallenberg said. "He can't do that."

"He can do that, and he has done it," I replied. "Ask him yourself."

Wallenberg did, and the man had no choice but to admit to his actions.

"I'm sorry," I told Wallenberg, "but you must agree this is going nowhere. We've got to call the merger off."

Wallenberg was not happy about that, but my priority was securing beneficial opportunities for Volvo, and that meant I had to strike while the iron was hot. The Volvo-Saab iron had cooled beyond the point of being malleable. And I had another venture I was eager to pursue. With the Volvo-Saab union officially dead by the middle of 1978, I made my first trip to Norway to meet with their prime minister, to begin talks of the Volvo-Norway alliance that Swedish industrialists, including their top dog Marcus Wallenberg, moved hard against.

Perhaps a year or so after the Norway deal was scuttled, in 1981, Wallenberg telephoned me again.

"Pehr," he said, "I would like you to have lunch with me."

"Lunch?" I asked. "Who else would be there? Big party?"

"No, Pehr," he said. "Only you. I'd like to speak to you alone."

I was a little curious, and even a little flattered, so I accepted his invitation.

We greeted one another pleasantly and with requisite formality, then sat down to eat. It is not often that I am caught off guard, but I was truly taken aback when he said, "Pehr, I would like you to succeed me."

I met his eye and waited for him to continue.

"I'm getting older," he told me. "And I want you to take over after I'm gone. I want you to be the head of the businesses, of all of it."

So the Wallenbergs had helped sabotage my work, but Marcus Wallenberg still wanted me to succeed. I knew that by way of his approach to me, he was acknowledging the potential of my Norway project and the fact that I had created something unprecedented; and though it remained unspoken, it was clear to me that he regretted his part in its failure. And I still harbored some negative feelings about the outcome. The mere fact of the organized opposition was endemic of something larger in Sweden, compounded by the subterfuge and lack of guts to make a public stand.

And yet the very fact that Wallenberg was asking me to succeed him did show some guts, as it was a move entirely lacking in subterfuge, and demonstrated a willingness to buck the establishment if he believed it was necessary for the well-being of his companies.

My response was intuitive—I felt no need to weigh the pros and cons, or devise hypothetical projections for the future, or mull over whether I was up to the task. The fact that Wallenberg asked was evidence that he knew I had the skills and the drive the job required. He had decided I was competent enough, therefore I didn't have any doubts that I would be able to do it.

"I won't give up my position at Volvo," I told him. "Presuming that is not an issue, then my answer is yes. I would like to succeed you."

He did not look surprised or gratified, nor was such emotion necessary. He knew I would accept his offer, just as I knew I would the moment the words left his lips.

We had several private meetings to discuss the logistics of the move. My agreement remained contingent on my retaining my position with Volvo, to which Wallenberg agreed. He then organized a dinner with all of his lieutenants, to be held at his family home, the Villa Tacka Udden.

The mansion was a French Renaissance-style villa, imposing with its elaborate towers, turrets, and steeply pitched roof. The villa was built on a small island on part of the old royal hunting grounds on the outskirts of Stockholm. The home was acquired in the late 1800s by Wallenberg's grandfather, A.O. Wallenberg, founder of Stockholm's Enskilda Bank. To approach and enter that house was to be palpably reminded of the money, power, and history of the family. Its significance was not lost on me.

I was led to a formal reception room, where the top executives of his empire, some twenty of them, had already assembled. Wallenberg had one surviving son—Peter Sr. His older son Marc had taken his own life in 1971, at the age of forty-seven.

Most of the other bosses at that time were not family members, but rather hired professional managers. Wallenberg directed me to sit on the sofa next to him, which was against the wall beneath twin portraits of K.A. and Alice Wallenberg. With a few short words he directed the others so that they were standing in a semicircle around us. Wallenberg didn't waste any time getting to the point.

He began by saying, "Well, you'll soon understand why PG is here. I've asked him to succeed me. And he has agreed."

There was no audible reaction in the room—no polite clapping or murmured response. There was nothing but dead silence. Wallenberg's people were unified in their facial expressions—every one of them looked flabbergasted and apprehensive. But just as there was no audible hint of polite support, there was absolutely no display of dissent, not even subtly. They were stunned, perplexed, and entirely unhappy with Wallenberg's announcement. But it was a fait accompli, and they accepted it as such.

After that evening, preliminary actions were taken to set the stage for my eventual takeover. But when Wallenberg became ill, we put things on the back burner to give him time to recover. But he didn't recover. In November of 1982 after suffering a heart attack, Marcus Wallenberg died.

His death was unexpected, and I was sorry to see him ago. My feelings about him were complicated and included many things I didn't like. He was at heart an industrialist, and by profession a banker, and a very powerful one. His view and approach to business were very different than his brother Jacob's had been, and that difference was one of the primary factors in Jacob's walking away from the family, business and all.

He could be very hypocritical, talking a good game about the importance of doing good in society. His power was such that he exerted a real influence on Sweden's society, but the reality is that he had no real interest in bestowing that society with charitable deeds. He also had many qualities that I must say that I thought were very good. I admired his tremendous confidence, and his leadership style as very tough taskmaster. I knew that he would never have turned to me unless he resolutely believed I would be his equal as a leader.

But with his death, those plans were permanently retired. I did not get along with his son Peter, and knew he was someone with whom I could not work. Even if I had liked Peter a great deal, with the death of Marcus, there was no inclination or reason for the Wallenbergs to continue drawing me into their clan.

I've been asked why Marcus Wallenberg made this request of me—what it was that he saw in me that his own team of people all lacked. I don't know—I certainly didn't ask him. He was not a person who thought it was necessary to verbalize his feelings about one's positive attributes. He was not that type of person to butter someone up, which was fine with me. He was also ambitious about gaining power in a way that few people are, or many aspire to but fail.

I had more than enough to keep me busy at Volvo, where I continued to do what I felt was necessary to create a sustainable future for Volvo. The scuttling of the Norway deal left a bad taste in my mouth, but I had no intention of allowing it to curtail my vision moving forward. Knowing that diversification was one of the keys to sustainability, I had led Volvo in acquiring interests in a variety of sectors, including the food industry, medical technology and pharmaceuticals, and finance, easing the burden of being interrelated with the ups and downs of any single industry.

Over a decade after the proposed Norway venture, another opportunity arose. This time it was for a fruitful alliance between Volvo and the French automobile company Renault. We had been working with Renault since 1990, and I began to negotiate with its CEO to create a merger between our two companies. Renault was state-owned, and a condition of the merger was that the company would become privatized. Legislation was created to prepare for that, but it did not dissuade the fear in Sweden that France would retain what is known as a "golden share" after privatization, somehow opening the doorway to the French taking control of the company. The merger would create one of the three biggest automotive groups in the world, of which Volvo would in effect hold 35 percent, but the naysayers had already begun to chatter.

This time, I might have seen the writing on the wall months before the conclusion had I felt reason to look. The press coverage was as intensive and alarmist as it had been with the Norway deal, but I also became aware that personal attacks against me were growing more intense. At a general meeting of the company in May, the press surrounded me as I got out of my car, peppering me with questions not about the merger, but about the personal benefits I was accorded as Volvo's CEO, such as my use of the company jet, and the corporate flat in New York. Even my own board seemed more concerned with discussing my salary and lifestyle than with discussing the details of the merger.

Though I'd personally witnessed the cost of Marcus Wallenberg's blind trust in the loyalty and support of management (when they had neither), I did not turn a skeptical eye on my own people. My senior executive, Soren Gyll, professed complete support for the fusion, issuing a company-wide letter endorsing the union and declaring that Volvo must take full advantage of it. But shareholder support continued to erode, and this kind of mass doubt does not begin in a vacuum—it has to be incited. There is always a source.

Analysts both during and after the buildup believed that at the heart of the matter was the fear that something uniquely Swedish would be vitiated or tainted in French hands. Although even the suggestion is ridiculous, it is the very kind of provocation that can ignite fear and powerful sentiment that overrides common sense and the recognition of what is genuinely good, versus what is clearly bad. We need look no farther than the simplistic "Make America Great Again" slogan wielded so frequently by Donald Trump—which by leveraging the fear incited by the word "again," got voters to believe that the greatness of the country and national identity had been snatched from them by foreigners.

With the negative feelings mounting, I called an impromptu meeting to take the corporate temperature as best I could. The outcome left no doubt whatsoever that there was a vocal and unapologetic group of executives who wanted Volvo to back out of the deal. I was in the midst of a full-scale revolt.

There was nothing ambiguous in the result. The majority of Swedish industry came out against the deal. Even as it became clear that the French Parliament favored the union, the merger was dead. My vision had failed. And it wasn't just the merger grinding to a halt. I was done. Done with Volvo, done with Sweden. I was fed up with being dominated by industrialist gangs, fed up with the ease with which people became fearful of a deal that would have created one of the three biggest automotive groups in world. I was fed up with a corporate culture that repeatedly demonstrated its willingness to cut off its nose to spite its face. I was tired of pettiness, of clandestine strategies, of short-termism, and most of all I was tired of the epidemic of dishonesty and corruption. No longer seeing through a glass darkly, I saw posturing and self-interest in every direction.

As I've said before, I didn't want anything from Volvo. I didn't want an exit package. I didn't want a golden handshake. I didn't even want a farewell ceremony, with all its incumbent duplicity and white lies. I was done, and I just wanted to close the door. I wasted no time in announcing my resignation.

I don't feel it necessary to compare the unraveling of the Norway deal to that of the Renault merger—it was enough that the sum total of the defeats was a clear signal to me that I had to move on. I will say that I had not developed a sufficient barometer for deceit. So when Soren Gyll, for example, supported the merger, signed the prospectus, and even sent a letter of endorsement to the employees, it did not occur to me to suspect he was talking out of both sides of his mouth (which of course, he was). At the press conference after that meeting and the announcement of my resignation, I expressed my deep disappointment that the project would not be fulfilled, saying, "In this period of restructuring in the automotive industry I think we need a stronger structure than Volvo can provide on a stand-alone basis." As to the reasons for the deal's collapse, I simply said that "business issues have been mixed with political and social ones…and the massive and often aggressive debate has created a powerful pressure on Volvo's social fabric...Management has not quite been able to resist these pressures." Indeed, management had not even been able to resist creating those same pressures.

The subtle but pervasive mistrust of my country I first felt as a child now rooted itself firmly in my consciousness. Processing those feelings openly was painful—and the shape of my misgivings became more an acknowledgment what I had lost—which was faith. I had lost faith in Sweden. And where had the Sweden in which I *did* have faith gone? I don't know. Perhaps in my lifetime it was always a distant memory.

I'm no historian, but in my opinion, Sweden's watershed moment took place in the early nineteenth century, when the Frenchman Jean Baptiste Bernadotte came to be the King of Sweden. He was not particularly interested in the country. Sweden's King Charles VXXX had just died suddenly and unexpectedly of a stroke. Priority was placed on finding a new king that Napoleon would not find objectionable. Bernadotte was, according to Napoleon, the only general who won battles. What kind of grounds are those on which to elect a king? Though my analysis may be faulty, I've come to believe that Bernadotte's choice as Sweden's crown prince marks the moment when the country began to move in the wrong direction. He was the turning point for Sweden.

Some things endure. I will never lose the sense of pleasure and pride of being made head of Volvo at thirty-six—and helping the company to grow tenfold in twenty-three years. Nor will I ever lose the feeling of sadness that once I had gone, Volvo became a target designed to offer no resistance to disarmament. By the year 2000, Volvo had been reduced to approximately 35 percent of the size it had been when I left it. They sold everything, including the car business, which Ford bought for $6.5 billion. But Ford simply couldn't manage it, and just a decade later, Ford sold Volvo to the Chinese group Zhejiang Geely for $1.8 billion. That represents a loss of a staggering 72 percent. For me, that was nothing short of tragic.

Volvo was a company that was grown in a single country and was a source of tremendous national pride. When I was its head, I could see far enough down the road to know what had to be done to safeguard the Volvo we knew and loved long into the future. And twice my efforts were thwarted, due in some part to Swedes' resistance of partnering with neighboring countries in the EU. Today, the Volvo car company as we knew it no longer exists. It's unthinkable. It is also absolutely consistent with the attitudes and the behavior of Swedish industrialists and my own colleagues in the 1970s and '80s.

Why say no to Renault? With the hindsight of history, I think many onetime detractors would have a hard time answering that question. Of the dire circumstances it was predicted might come to pass—of France taking its golden share and rendering Volvo vulnerable to its Frankish influence—how do those fears look now, compared to the prospect of passing a starving company to the Americans, who mismanage two-thirds of its value away before passing it to the Chinese?

Why say no to Norway? Thirty-five years later people still talk about the lost deal and what a shame it was. In those years, the influx of oil money has transformed Norway. The oil concessions and gas Volvo and Sweden would have received are equivalent in today's terms to $85 billion, two or three times the value of the entire Volvo group. With that success, Volvo and Sweden would have raced ahead of our neighbors on the Scandinavian peninsula and past many European nation-states as well. What that means to me is that Volvo's future, and its legacy as a Swedish company operating in Sweden, would have been secured. Instead, that security was never realized because of lack of vision, short-termism, and a me-first mentality in the Swedish business community.

I know that it can be difficult to gain a clear perspective of the trees when standing in the middle of the forest. With the distance of time and space, things become much clearer. In the United States, this same kind of short-termism and me-first mentality in the political and corporate spheres has reached grotesque proportions. Top executives make seven-figure salaries while middle-class paychecks shrink. Empowered by vast wealth, those controlling the biggest businesses have made alarming inroads in customizing the current administration to maximize corporate profits and minimize worker benefits and environmental protection.

As the president whom those corporations supported remains (at the time of this writing) in office, he is systematically dismantling every protective regulation seen as inconvenient to big business, while defying the justice system and working to reorganize it so that his considerable criminal activities, both as president and as a business owner manipulating the system for his own profit, will not only go unpunished but will be effectively sanctioned. Few foreigners have any doubt about the extent of the greed and corruption in Washington, nor do they have trouble imagining how cataclysmic itw effects on the rest of the world might be. No reasonable person observing the Republican Party as they collectively remain silent in the face of each catastrophe, or evincing their willingness to lie through their teeth to defend

Trump, could conclude that the GOP is doing anything but protecting itself at any cost. Few can argue that the GOP has demonstrated it is willing to sacrifice Americans' human rights, health care, education, their liberty, pursuit of happiness, and even their lives, just to gamble on the possibility that Trump might succeed in breaking the democracy, which would allow them to remain in power. It's almost too horrific to contemplate.

And yet, Sweden has demonstrated those very same impulses on a smaller scale.

There was a time when I could not have imagined feeling disappointed with or angry at my home country (just as I imagine millions of Americans could not have imagined feeling disgusted and betrayed by the USA). But my vision has never changed. It doesn't take much to set a country on the wrong path. And it doesn't take much for that path to make some unexpected turns into very unpleasant territory.

The loss of integrity, the loss of the ability to communicate, and the loss of openness that transcends borders—these are three faces of oppression, of fascism, of dictatorship. The prioritization of me/us, the willingness to be knowingly dishonest, and the belief that we have been wrongfully robbed of our own great yesterday—these are also the faces of oppression, fascism, and dictatorship.

So while I'm not comparing the failure of the Norwegian project to the transgressions of America's politicians, I am pointing out that they stem from the same basic things. In *Manufacturing Consent*, Noam Chomsky wrote:

> As long as some specialized class is in a position of authority, it is going to set policy in the special interests that it serves.

> But the conditions of survival, let alone justice, require rational social planning in the interests of the community as a whole and, by now, that means the global community. The question is whether privileged elites should dominate mass-communication and should use this power as they tell us they must, namely, to impose necessary illusions, manipulate and deceive the stupid majority, and remove them from the public arena. The question, in brief, is whether democracy and freedom are values to be preserved or threats to be avoided. In this possibly terminal phase of human existence, democracy and freedom are more than values to be treasured, they may well be essential to survival.

Wise words and wise questions—ones I wish we had considered more closely and more carefully in 1979, and in 1993, and at many points in between and since.

CHAPTER NINE

Organization

Organization: *mid-15c., "act of organizing," from Middle French organisation and directly from Medieval Latin organizationem (nominative organizatio), noun of action from past participle stem of organizare, from Latin organum "instrument, organ". Meaning "system, establishment" is from 1873.*

–Oxford English Dictionary

Several times in the course of my career, I have worked with the United Nations, primarily at the UN Office at Geneva (UNOG), and over the years I have been offered various positions, including one as deputy secretary-general. I have the greatest respect for the principles on which the UN was founded, but as early as the 1970s I came to believe that the UN was a hopeless organization. It has grown into a giant, a monster, a bureaucracy beyond belief.

The UN was founded in 1945, and its charter drawn up by representatives from all fifty states in the United Nations Conference on International Organization. The ideas and principles behind the UN were absolutely right, and the charter is fantastic. In that charter, there is a simple four-part summary of the purpose of the organization:

1. To maintain international peace and security, and to that end: to take effective collective measures for the prevention and removal of threats to the peace, and for the suppression of acts of aggression or other breaches of the peace, and to bring about by peaceful means, and in conformity with the principles of justice and international law, adjustment or settlement of international disputes or situations which might lead to a breach of the peace;
2. To develop friendly relations among nations based on respect for the principle of equal rights and self-determination of peoples, and to take other appropriate measures to strengthen universal peace;
3. To achieve international co-operation in solving international problems of an economic, social, cultural, or humanitarian character, and in promoting and encouraging respect for human rights and for fundamental freedoms for all without distinction as to race, sex, language, or religion; and
4. To be a center for harmonizing the actions of nations in the attainment of these common ends.

Unfortunately, the organization has long since lost sight of this vision, and has become a hotbed of corruption and paralysis, enmeshed in red tape. I came to this conclusion from direct experience. During a three-year period when I worked on and off with the UN Refugee Agency (the UNHCR) in the early 1990s, High Commissioner Sadako Ogata was always very pleased with the proposals I prepared for her. But when it came down to moving forward to execute them, she would tell me it wasn't possible. I heard this time and time again. The UNHCR was a large operation, employing about 3,000 people, with offices spread over two separate buildings, expensive to run and as cumbersome to operate as any typical oversize bureaucracy. No tax, no obligations—no work.

One day, I sat down with Sadako and said, "There is one thing you really should do. You have two separate buildings here in Geneva, with about 1,500 people in each one. Nothing can really get done, and it costs so much to maintain, there's no money left to implement programs. Get rid of one of the buildings, and lay off half of your total staff, or send them out into the field. You'd be left with more than enough to run your end."

She gave me a lovely smile, then said, "I could never even imagine doing that."

"Well, then I'm afraid my service to you is over," was my response.

That was really the point where I lost all hope for the UN. I was so dismayed by what I'd seen of its internal workings that to even consider taking a post there would forever remain impossible. They spend so much maintaining the bloated status quo there is rarely any money left to fund programming. Their efficiency level is so low it is unbelievable. From what I witnessed, what they are best at is simply sitting in their offices chatting and lecturing others. The "Big Five" (United States, France, Britain, China, and Russia), as the five permanent nation members of the UN Security Council are called, have a chokehold on the voting process by way of their power to veto. I find it absolutely intolerable that they have rendered the organization untouchable, as if it is something sacred.

I don't believe the current organization is salvageable. The UN is now over seventy years old—neither people nor administrative systems are apt to change at that age. The infrastructure is overbuilt, the fixed costs are too high, and the corruption is too endemic. If I had the power and the influence, I would shut the whole thing down and start a new organization that is at most 10 percent of the size of the original. I would give it the same guiding principles and values laid out in the UN charter, but they would be implemented by a group that was much smaller, more efficient, and hence more effective. It a simple proposition, but it is also highly unlikely ever to be realized.

A 2016 article in the *Economist* observes that, "Despite the UN's glaring faults, deplored ever more vociferously by its critics, most reforms are likely to be blocked. The Big Five are still prone to veto any dilution of their power. The world needs a well-run UN, led by someone clever and tough yet idealistic. Sadly, it probably will not get it."

To get an understanding of how deeply ingrained the UN's level of bureaucratic dysfunction has become, simply take a look at their secretary-generals over the last four decades. They are an underwhelming, mediocre, and occasionally outright corrupt group. I would argue that the UN has not had an effective secretary-general since Dag Hammerskjold, who was killed in the middle of his term in a 1961 plane crash. Since then, most of them have been lame ducks—not by accident, but by design of the Big Five, none of whom want to see anyone with power in the top UN position.

This kind of excessive and self-crippling bureaucratic bloat is by no means unique to the United Nations, nor are private organizations immune to this syndrome—Bilderberg, the Club of Rome, and the Davos World Economic Forum, to name a few, have suffered deterioration and lapsed into impotence over time. In the most generous view, they have become places where people gather more to hear themselves talk than with any serious intention of taking action. In the case of Davos, at least, I can attest as someone who was there at its start that it began as something very different than it is today.

I came to Davos in something of a roundabout way, following a series of events that began in the late 1960s, when I was thirty-two or thirty-three years old. I was then still working at the Skandia insurance company, and shortly would become its president and CEO. Skandia's chairman wanted me to go through the Harvard Owner/President Management Program, which is a global executive leadership program. But my chairman was told by the Harvard OPM representative that I did not qualify as I fell short of their minimum age requirement, which was thirty-eight. The chairman was irate, and responded to them that I was going to become Skandia's CEO, and anyway, was it not his job to determine whether or not I was too young for something?

Ultimately, I went to Centre d'Etudes Industrielles in Geneva, which was offering a new program in leadership that was structurally similar to Harvard's OPM. Once there, however, I found myself quickly growing bored, and found little in the program to challenge me. After two weeks, I impulsively told the CDI dean that I wasn't getting enough out of the program, and that I had decided to go home. The dean implored me to reconsider, candidly telling me that I was their top student, and that my early departure from their very first leadership program could scuttle the entire venture. I reconsidered my departure, and also gave some thought to how my chairman might react to my quitting mid-course. Therefore, I saw the course through, and I knew that the dean was relieved and grateful.

Nonetheless, I was surprised when he asked me, immediately after the program was over, if I wanted to join the school's board of directors. I was still not terribly impressed with their leadership program. However, they were offering a number of seminars on their schedule that looked interesting to me. So I accepted their invitation, and joined the Centre d'Etude Industrielles' board. The board was just beginning a study involving the creation of an international symposium that would be based in Switzerland, for the reason of the country's well-known neutrality. I was asked to be a part of that study, and to help to design a symposium that would invite politicians, business leaders, and other individuals who were known in the world to discuss and debate the most current and relevant sociopolitical issues of the day. The symposium was separated from the Centre d'Etudes Industrielles and made an independent foundation so that the economic success or failure of one was not tied to the other.

The new institution was essentially a success from the very beginning. It was the first program of its kind in Europe. The location was accessible and had sufficiently good infrastructure and amenities to support many visitors. When the first symposium was scheduled, it happened to coincide with a tour of Europe that Paul Volcker was making. Volcker was US President Nixon's Undersecretary for the Treasury for International Monetary Affairs, and the US had just dropped the gold standard that links the value of national currency to the value of gold. To mitigate the concern over what was widely referred to as the Nixon Shock, Volcker undertook a tour of European capitals to deliver a series of lectures to the public that would provide both explanation and reassurance in the wake of the move.

Volcker was invited to speak at the inaugural symposium event, which at that time was being called the European Management

Forum, and I was asked to participate as one of the panelists. He and I both made speeches and then the two of us had a moderated debate. In spite of (or perhaps because of) the fact that we had differing views on the subject, we took an instant liking to one another. The year was 1971, and Paul Volcker and I became friends and remained close until his death in 2019.

Volcker had a remarkable career—a model of a permanent civil servant who played different roles, serving under four presidents and becoming the chairman of the Federal Reserve. He established the Volcker Commission, which investigated a number of World War Two-era Swiss bank accounts created by Jewish people during the Holocaust, containing assets that were never returned to the survivors or their heirs. He also headed a commission investigating allegations of UN corruption in the Iraqi Food for Oil program.

That first EMF symposium was quite well attended, and within a few years, the program had become extremely popular. It was a new venture with an enormous audience, and people were quite meticulous in what they were saying. The concept that the neutrality of Switzerland would make it an attractive location proved to be well founded. It had a huge budget, enough to bring in world-class speakers, and a growing number of people from corporations all over the world wanted to join. After a while it was quite easy to draw superstars. I couldn't take credit for any part of it—other than my role on the board and my participation in the decision to start the symposium.

In 1987, the program changed its name to the World Economic Forum, and its much-vaunted annual winter meeting referred to by the name of the Swiss mountain resort town where it is held—Davos. I was invited back a few times by the Davos chairman, Klaus Schwab, who is still there at the time of this writing, over forty-five years later.

Born in Germany, Schwab began his career as a professor, I think without great success. He was considered a better organizer than he was an educator. I think it was Schwab's idea to break the symposium business into a foundation. He is quite a renowned figure in the world of conferences today. I didn't really take to Schwab on a personal level, but he was well suited to be an administrator, and has proven to be a real entrepreneur in running the Davos symposium. With its soaring popularity, Davos became increasingly elite, almost grotesquely so. Today, Davos is a supreme status symbol—it is a conference where "everyone who is anyone" attends, a reputation so widely known and accepted that Donald Trump felt it necessary to show up in 2018, lest the world suspect he did not occupy the top tier of all elites.

Exclusive and elite organizations are unsurprisingly distanced from the reality of life for most people. They are also more prone to the idea that the have-nots find themselves in that position through flawed character or poor decision-making. As Nigerian LGBT advocate Adebisi Ademola Alimi wrote in a 2017 article for the Independent, "Arriving in Davos, it was very clear to me from day one that 90 percent [of the people] there are disconnected from the people of the world they are trying to save and, frankly, [are] more interested in proving to each other their own worth."

For the average or even above-average person, the exorbitant price of admission is simply prohibitive. WEF membership and a basic-level entry ticket to the Davos event are a staggering $70,000, and 80 percent of attendants are white men. To maintain its ultra-elite reputation, Davos will likely become more expensive in the future, not less. Given its trajectory, it is hard to imagine how any substantive and beneficial program for the masses could possibly come of a symposium that is effectively acting as a forum for the wealthiest citizens of the world to assert their status.

At the risk of repeating myself, I don't believe that any organization can independently endure in keeping with the vision of the individuals who founded it. There must be active and consistent input by directors or formally appointed supervisors to safeguard the original vision, and to prevent the organization from veering off course. The Davos vision is described on its website as follows: "The Forum strives in all its efforts to demonstrate entrepreneurship in the global public interest while upholding the highest standards of governance. Moral and intellectual integrity is at the heart of everything it does." In reality, I think this institution has come to the point where it is governed by one thing: money.

Today, Davos overshadows its own organizational body of the World Economic Forum, like the tail that wags the dog. In a 2012 *New Yorker* article, Nick Paumgarten wrote, "Today, the W.E.F., with lavish headquarters overlooking Lake Geneva, has more than four hundred employees, who churn out reports and convene conferences around the world. You get the sense that they sometimes regret the attention paid to Davos, and even to Schwab. 'Davos is less and less important to the organization,' Adrian Monck, the W.E.F.'s media director, told me. 'It's no longer the best example of what we can do.'"

I can think of many groups in which talk never gives rise to anything substantial, and I can think of few from which substantial change has come. Most organizations probably fall somewhere between the two extremes. Some of them I have joined, some I have declined to join, and occasionally there has been one I have felt it necessary to simply quit. Bohemian Grove falls into the last of those categories.

I was invited to go to Bohemian Grove by David Rockefeller, with whom I'd been friends since our first meeting in 1971 in Gothenburg. Both he and his brother Nelson Rockefeller were longtime members of the Bohemian Club in San Francisco—a private club known for its roster of high-powered politicians and captains of industry. What the club is most famous for is a summer gathering it hosts every year for its members and invited guests, at an encampment in a 2,700-acre property in the redwood forest north of San Francisco. Both the property and the summer camp are referred to as Bohemian Grove.

The Bohemian Club and the Grove were established in the late nineteenth century, originally as a gathering place for journalists, who referred to themselves as "bohemians." There are probably not many journalists currently on the membership roster, but what Bohemian Grove does have in copious amounts is the lore, rumors, and conspiracy theories that surround it. It has been called an organization of Satanists who practice human sacrifice, a modern-day cabal of Illuminati, a den of immorality, and the world's biggest party for powerful men. Presidents and ex-presidents, including Eisenhower, Nixon, Ford, Reagan, and Bush (41), have been guests there. The exaggerated atmosphere of secrecy (especially surrounding the traditional rituals performed there) fuels the many theories about Bohemian Grove that are always making the rounds. Immortalized on an Oval Office tape recording, Richard Nixon told John Ehrlichman that, "The Bohemian Grove which I attend from time to time...is the most faggy goddamned thing you could ever imagine, with that San Francisco crowd. I can't shake hands with anybody from San Francisco."

David Rockefeller invited me to go to Bohemian Grove for three consecutive summers as his guest. I will say I have never seen anything like it. There were huts built up in trees, to which you climbed. David had a fairly big treehouse pavilion, and somehow managed to get a grand piano into it. He would invite pianists to come and perform there. The pavilion was quite elegant, especially when compared to the sleeping quarters, which were primitive. They were essentially little bunks, like you might find on a ship. There was quite a dichotomy between the austere sleeping quarters and the luxurious pavilion, where you could sit enjoying a glass of very fine wine while listening to a concert pianist playing Chopin.

There was a lake at the center of the compound, where a forty-foot sculpture of an owl stands—the owl being the symbol of the Bohemian Club. Guests would assemble there for lakeside presentations and lectures. One of the first that I attended was a talk given by Warren Buffett. After a presentation, you would be invited to various different huts or cabins, some small and some quite ostentatious, where you mixed with former presidents, cabinet members, tycoons, billionaires—an extraordinary mix of people. Henry Kissinger was often there, as was David's and my mutual friend Paul Volcker.

In my recollection, there were no women on the compound except for the ones who served food at the canteens. And in spite of a guest list that included some of the world's most powerful and wealthy men, there was a great deal about Bohemian Grove that in my opinion ranged from the eccentric to the bizarre. For example, there were no toilets at the encampment. When someone had to pee, they just picked a spot outside—often one of the redwood trees—and there they went. There were also the previously mentioned ritualistic ceremonies such as the opening Cremation of Care ceremony, which is performed on a stage in front of the massive owl statue, complete with robed attendants and a mannequin burned in effigy and launched on a raft across the lake. After three years I decided it was just too bizarre—I couldn't stand it anymore. Though I had met many heads of state and government officials and industrialists at Bohemian Grove, as an institution it really just wasn't for me. I decided I would not accept another invitation to the camp.

Though I'd had enough of Bohemian Grove, I remained as fond of David Rockefeller as ever. David was a remarkable person—someone who could be described as a Renaissance man. He was a real force in business, politics, and the art world, and was one of the truly great philanthropists of his time. When he died in 2017 at the age of 101, his *New York Times* obituary said, "His stature was greater than any corporate title might convey.... His influence was felt in Washington and foreign capitals, in the corridors of New York City government, in art museums, in great universities and in public schools. Mr. Rockefeller could well be the last of a less and less visible family to have cut so imposing a figure on the world stage... he was a force in global financial affairs and in his country's foreign policy. He was received in foreign capitals with the honors accorded a chief of state."

He was extremely interested in art, literature, and music, and supported the arts at a level few others ever equaled. When David committed to a charitable organization, whether an existing one, or one of his own making, he invested himself in it entirely. His five siblings all shared that trait to some degree. David was the brother of former New York Governor Nelson Rockefeller, and grandson of industrialist and Standard Oil and Chase Manhattan founder John D. Rockefeller—one of the richest Americans in the country's history. The Rockefeller are a highly respected American dynasty and over the years have given away a great deal of their wealth in support of art, education, and conservationism. One of the best-known institutions they created is New York's Museum of Modern Art, of which David was the chairman emeritus.

When I first met David in 1971, his official reason for the trip to Sweden was that he had been invited by some Gothenburg city officials to attend an international festival. But when he came to visit me at Volvo the following day, he told me the real reason he had come was to meet me. I found him to be very gracious and pleasant, and invited him to join me for lunch in my new office. During that lunch, he asked me to become a member of Chase Manhattan Bank's International Advisory Committee. Of course, I accepted this invitation. It was quite an illustrious group of iconic industrialists, and though I never feel that I shrink in the company of others, in that case I almost did. David maintained the group with great attention, and as a result, I remained on the committee for many years—from 1971 until 1995. That is a testament to David Rockefeller.

In spite of their enormous wealth and the reputation of the Rockefeller name, David and his wife, Peggy, were both modest and unassuming people. They were avid sailors, hikers, and cyclists, and truly delighted in nature. They also had a monumental and unrivaled art collection, including a vast number of nineteenth- and twentieth-century European and American paintings. In the foreword to the MOMA catalog of an exhibition of their collection, David wrote, "We never bought a painting with a view towards 'forming a collection' or to 'fill out a series,' but simply because, in the end, we couldn't resist it. Through this rather unscientific process, we have been fortunate to have surrounded ourselves with beautiful works of art that have given us unending and increasing pleasure as we have lived with them over time."

My wife and I had David and Peggy as guests in our house in Sweden, and at a very primitive cottage in the north of Norway where we all went salmon fishing for three days. Peggy was very dynamic and lively, with a wonderful sense of humor. She was a dedicated environmentalist and founding board member of the American Farmland Trust, and on the board of managers of

New York's Botanical Gardens. She also had a project buying up undeveloped islands in Maine and making them nature preserves.

They in turn had us as guests a number of times, at their upstate New York farmhouse, Four Winds, at Ringing Point in Maine's Seal Harbor, and at their Manhattan townhouse. They spent much of their time at their big country home, Hudson Pines, in Cantico Hills. When they had their golden wedding anniversary celebration at Hudson Pines in 1990, they invited us to attend. My wife couldn't go, but I attended.

Hudson Pines is a Georgian-style mansion designed by the American architect Mott Schmidt, who had a long relationship with the family and had been commissioned to design twelve Rockefeller homes over several generations of the family. The anniversary dinner was held at the house which overlooked the Hudson River. A tent was set up on the lawn for the party. There were perhaps a hundred guests there, including many big personalities and very rich people. I had very little money and was not part of that worldly society. But David had announced that I was their guest of honor, and as such I was expected to make a speech. I was not prepared, so I had to improvise. Fortunately, that is one of the things I can do without losing track of the subject or coughing or dithering. It was quite an occasion, and I was very touched by the fact that I was guest of honor.

The network of friends David acquired internationally in his role as a banker and as a statesman was as unparalleled as his art collection. In addition to belonging to organizations such as the Bilderberg Group and the Bohemian Club, David was one of the founders in 1973 (along with Paul Volcker and Alan Greenspan) of the Trilateral Commission, a nonpartisan symposium of private citizens created to foster closer cooperation between the US, Europe, and Japan. The Trilateral Commission is still in existence today. I believe it has outlived its usefulness, and at some point I told David that. I explained my belief that one should never institutionalize such a grouping. It comes to resemble a bunch of old friends meeting and spending all their time chatting and one-upping each other. I told him that in my view, the Trilateral Commission should be abandoned. David was always interested in others' opinions, but he listened to everything I had to say. He wasn't offended, but he didn't agree with my view either, and the Trilateral Commission endured.

Remarkable organizations consist of remarkable people; a Paul Volcker or a David Rockefeller is worth a thousand boards of mediocrity and a million rule books. We recognize that individuals have life spans; they peak and decline; they make their contributions and eventually stand aside for others. It is the rare organization that does likewise. The founders of organizations—the United Nations, the World Economic Forum, the Trilateral Commission, even Bohemian Grove—are often men and women of vision and commitment whose ethos is more or less successfully embodied in a set of principles and of procedures that can outlast them. But no organization, ultimately, is better than the people who comprise it. It is a rare foundation or seminar or business or governmental agency (or indeed a government) that continually attracts the best, most committed and creative men and women, people who can revise and reinvigorate its fundamental vision and its systems of operation. Species evolve through development and the trial and error of their individual components; human organizations usually cannot. When we have become wise enough to learn to apply the principles of our own best natures to all our communal efforts, then we may create organizations that are as enduringly effective, and as precious, as the singular genius of one indispensable human being.

CHAPTER TEN

Integrity

Integrity: *from Latin integritas; wholeness, entireness, completeness, chastity, purity.*

–Oxford English Dictionary

Over the course of this book, I have shared my personal experiences of both exceptional individuals and exceptional organizations. Whatever qualities I have observed that have made them exceptional, two are always present. The first is an integrity that is consistently manifested in thought and communicated in speech and action; the second is an unwavering vision that is the ongoing goal in every action. An individual can maintain integrity and vision in the absence of an organization, but the converse is not true. No organization can continue on course over time in the absence of a like-minded leader. I've also observed that of all the characteristics inherent to a great or powerful leader, such as courage and commitment, there is one that is paramount, and that in and of itself can make a good leader into a great one, and that is the ability to communicate effectively with one's constituents, workers, or followers.

In Europe and America, social and political developments of the last several years have brought us to a watershed moment in the history of the world's two greatest democratic entities. The EU and the US government are both in a state of disorder and vulnerability. The US government took less than a year to succumb to paralysis in the wake of the successive concussions caused by the Trump administration. America's most integral institutions have been scuttled or sabotaged, with newly appointed leaders who are often openly in opposition to the group's core visions. Its justice system is under siege, and numerous campaign and administration figures have been indicted on multiple criminal counts. For the first time in history, an American president is conducting his business from the Oval Office as an unindicted coconspirator in a criminal matter. Embroiled in a constitutional crisis, it is unclear if the American system of democracy as we know it is going to survive.

In Europe, the EU is facing a growing upheaval of its own. Nationalism is on the rise and right-wing political parties are winning larger electoral gains in several nation-states. In Italy an antiestablishment group and a right-wing party have formed a government coalition, in Austria the far-right Freedom Party came close to winning a presidential election, and in Hungary the authoritarian and extremist Victor Orban recently won his fourth term as prime minister—declaring that the day of "liberal democracy" has come to an end. In Sweden, nationalist support is approaching 20 percent and support for the Social Democrats has fallen to 28.3 percent, a low not seen since before the Second World War.

The dream of an enlightened and humanistic world seems (for the moment) to be crushed. Greed and wealth have conquered the idea of a fair state. Will it reappear at all? If the growing trend of total disregard for citizens continues, war will likely erupt. We are in the midst of an earthquake that is shaking our most vital infrastructures—we hope to live through it and redesign them to withstand another shock.

What's going to happen? It's a question I'm often asked. It's also a question I often ask myself. When my young daughter is old enough to step out into the world on her own, what kind of world might she find herself in? It is human nature to want to know what is going to happen in order to feel that one can at the very least make preparations. I am not a fortune-teller, and for the most part I prefer to share what I know about the world through my direct experiences, rather than to offer conjecture and hypothesis. But like everyone else, I'm working to come to an understanding of how and why both the United States and the European Union have become so vulnerable, to what extent human leadership has contributed to that state, and most importantly, what we can learn in order to make changes to both institutions to avoid the return of this kind of disorder. To do that, we have to look at their beginnings, or the core around which each organization has been built.

The European Union is the vastly younger of the two. It was formally established in 1951 as the European Coal and Steel Community, following a call by French Foreign Minister Robert Schuman that is today called the Schuman Declaration, which opened with the statement, "World peace cannot be safeguarded without the making of creative efforts proportionate to the dangers which threaten it." The European Coal and Steel Community (ECSC) was founded by six countries—Belgium, West Germany, France, Italy, Luxembourg, and the Netherlands—to regulate their industrial production after the Second World War. But the broader purpose of the ECSC went far beyond heavy industry concerns. Europe still had a long way to go in recovering from the cataclysmic damage sustained in the Second World War. Rebuilding and recovering had to come in gradual steps, beginning with a foundation strong enough to sustain rapid growth in the future.

In Schuman's words, "Europe will not be made all at once, or according to a single plan. It will be built through concrete achievements which first create a de facto solidarity. The coming together of the nations of Europe requires the elimination of the age-old opposition of France and Germany. Any action taken must in the first place concern these two countries."

In simple terms, the ECSC's unified trans-European steel and coal market was conceived to act as a safeguard against Germany and France ever going to war again, by effectively making it impossible for any one of the member countries to manufacture weapons for use in waging war upon the others. Its other stated purposes, as Schuman worded it, included:

1. ...the setting up of common foundations for economic development as a first step in the federation of Europe;
2. ...the realization of the first concrete foundation of a European federation indispensable to the preservation of peace;
3. [to]...revitalize the whole European economy...[and] change the destinies of those regions which have long been devoted to the manufacture of munitions of war, of which they have been the most constant victims;
4. [to free]...movement of coal and steel between member countries...from all customs duty;
5. [its production]...offered to the world as a whole without distinction or exception, with the aim of contributing

to raising living standards and to promoting peaceful achievements;

6. ...to pursue the achievement of one of its essential tasks, namely, the development of the African continent.

Each of the above points makes it abundantly clear what the real reason was behind the formation of the ESCS and ultimately the European Union. Having survived the Second World War, these leaders were saying "never again," and actively working to design a historically unprecedented institution that would act as a guarantee of such into the future.

Gradually the ESCS recognized that more could be cooperatively accomplished if the field were wider. The group of six became a customs union called the European Economic Community, brought about by the 1957 Treaty of Rome (which would ultimately provide the constitutional core of the European Union).

By 1961, the founding six became a group of nine, with the addition of Ireland, Denmark, and Norway. The cooperation was successful and encouraging. The UK applied to join the association as well, but Charles de Gaulle exercised veto power and refused to let the "islanders" in, famously saying, "l'Angleterre, ce n'est plus grand chose" ("England is no longer a big thing"). The UK had to wait until 1973 when de Gaulle resigned.

In 1993 the EEC became the European Union, and a number of new nation-states became members and established the European Citizenship during the 1990s. I can find no better evidence of the brilliance of the EU's design than the fact that seventy years after its genesis in the Treaty of Rome, the EU has grown from six to twenty-eight nation members and comprises the biggest trading area in the world. Its creation is a revolutionary development in history, and it is a remarkable and unique achievement by sovereign nations accomplished without any armed conflicts—a borderless union where citizens can cross without passports and pay no duties. The only exception is the UK, where passports are necessary. (I see that as very typically British.)

There are now new tensions and strains on the EU. In a referendum that many believe should never have been offered, British citizens voted to withdraw from the EU to restore the independence and glory of their nation, in a move quickly dubbed Brexit. By most accounts, it is an overwhelmingly bad idea for the British to leave the union. They must on a practical level continue to participate in the unified economy—what they are relinquishing is any right to have a say in how that economy operates. Former Prime Minister Tony Blair called Brexit a "mistake of destiny." Via Brexit, the British have succeeded in creating a colossal mess for themselves, and even after their official departure date of January 31, 2020, a clear and viable strategy is still needed vis a vis their relationship with the EU as it pertains to trade, law enforcement, electrical and gas supply, and numerous other areas, as well as concrete plans for the nation's future.

Brexit has—essentially by default—spread uncertainty through the EU, with some members already suffering from a kind of EU fatigue stemming from the decision-making process that fosters "centralized decisions." Such sentiment is dangerously misguided. In a union of nation-states, by its very definition nothing can be decided without consensus. Centralized decisions are the sine qua non of the European Union. The advantages far outweigh such disadvantages—EU citizens have an unprecedented freedom of movement and are subject to no duties within the union. It is a fantastic example to the world—particularly when parts of Europe such as Poland, Hungary, and Austria are showing signs of becoming fascist again. As a person who has long known and understood the benefit of a unified European economy (and who directly experienced the Second World War and its aftermath), I find even the suggestion that the EU might not survive to be tragic.

Like all true democracies, the EU is broadly inclusive, and as such there are always antidemocratic tendencies within it. Some of the members must have disregarded their past suppression by Russia. Poland, Hungary, and the Czech Republic are examples, and their leaders are arrogant and impertinent and frequently test the patience of the council. Russia itself is a supremely manipulative dictatorship, and as such it poses a significant threat to the EU, a threat that will grow at the first sign of any cracks forming around the EU's edges.

Throughout the ebb and flow of individual national cycles, the areas of EU concern have been predictable and consistent. In addition to immigration, extremism in Africa and the Middle East, and controversial moves in China in claiming new territory, Russia often tops the list of threatening neighbors, as a country with strained resources and a vulnerable economy and structure that is prone to be moved to violence and destructive and brutal behavior.

In 2018 the European Union added a new unfriendly neighbor to the list—the United States of America. The categorization of the US as unfriendly to Europe is a stunning sociopolitical turnaround and gives a chilling example of how quickly and categorically a long-standing democratic institution can be hobbled by a single individual.

The revered American three-branch democracy with its system of checks and balances and its constitutional core was once seen as infallible. The election of Donald Trump changed that forever. Within months of his election, in actions including a series of executive orders, a barrage of statements and claims, and unrelenting streams of blatant lies in interviews, speeches, and tweets, Trump established that he intended to simply bypass both Congress and his own staff and do, say, and order more or less whatever he wanted (preferences and intentions that often changed from one extreme to the other and back again). He then reinforced his own actions with more lies that began with his insistence that the crowd at his inauguration was a record-setting 1.5 million, when it is plainly evident that only 250,000 attended.

In American politics, honesty and character are closely scrutinized. For many a politician, a single bald-faced lie or character lapse has been enough to scuttle a career. Americans found themselves completely unprepared to deal with a leader who lied on a daily basis, whilst simultaneously laying siege to the free press and the right of free speech. It is a tragic caricature of what a president can do. But somehow, his hold on power is sufficiently strong that his GOP colleagues, with a very few exceptions, refuse to revolt or even to speak out against him.

Donald Trump, who has no moral compass and operates with a severely limited understanding of facts, has nonetheless managed to acquire leadership power and hold on to it. What has paralyzed the country on a mass basis is people's very basic inability to handle the kind of sustained and unapologetic dishonesty he has unleashed. When a public figure is caught in a lie, we cannot see beyond it, and usually it is a foregone conclusion that the individual caught in that lie will step down. This American president's behavior has been different—he neither feels nor displays any sense of embarrassment or shame when faced with evidence that he has said something untrue. This is akin to an otherwise below average athlete who happens to be impervious to physical pain—unaffected by what would cripple anyone else, he has been able to continue unimpeded. I've previously said that the equation for an exceptionally great leader is integrity plus vision multiplied by communication that disseminates the value of ethics. Current events demonstrate an inverse version of this equation for an exceptionally dangerous leader: lack of integrity and tunnel vision multiplied by communication that disseminates the unimportance of ethics. When an individual who does not experience or acknowledge shame acquires power, their capacity for destruction is almost unlimited.

The US Constitution was brilliantly designed to be malleable over time. But you cannot fully safeguard against something that is impossible to imagine. The Constitution created governmental branches, checks and balances set to prevent a sitting president from making a successful power grab—this was something that could be imagined might happen one day. The Constitution does not prevent—or does not yet prevent—a president from firing or revoking security clearance for anyone in the Department of Justice who questions or investigates his actions; it does not even prevent a president from disregarding the Constitution altogether. What the Constitution does do is to provide a foundational basis for removing a president from office if he fails to carry out his job or is found guilty of high crimes and misdemeanors. The catch is that it requires human beings to put such a process in motion, and the human beings in Congress have shown absolutely no inclination to do so. This again is something the Constitution does not have a safeguard for, because it was unthinkable to the Founding Fathers that a democratically elected Congress would sit on their hands and look the other way throughout a corrupt and treasonous presidency. The writers of the Constitution had to make certain basic assumptions about the American people and presume they would all possess certain commonsense behaviors, just as the designer of a submarine hatch works with the basic assumption that the submarine captain will close the hatch before submerging.

What is now clear, however, is that there were also numerous invisible cracks in the American foundation that long predate the Trump era. The advent of the Trump base brought those flaws to the light. Extremism, the appearance of which had always largely been seen as a negative, suddenly received political and moral sanction from a presidential candidate and sitting president. Trump's political rallies were places where xenophobia, racism, misogyny, and homophobia could be publicly displayed, supported, and championed. This was a surprise to many people both in the US and abroad—that so many citizens, from average civilians to politicians—could behave so shamelessly.

I have great fondness for the US, many of my friends are American, and I've spent a great deal of time in the country. Nonetheless, it is difficult for me to understand how the right wing has garnered so much support and success in America, other than the fact that the wealthiest Americans support it to protect their own fortunes. The Tea Party is fueled first and foremost by money, and it is money that the party values above all else—any lobbyist knows the relationship between the special interests of wealthy constituents and the legislation that the Tea Party champions or opposes. It is perhaps the least complicated portion of the Trump base—the one motivated entirely by self-interest and short-termism in protecting one's own financial interests. But when immigration and racial and social issues are leveraged and inflamed, a new brand of short-termist conservative loudly and vocally emerges—the voter who is not wealthy, but who has been encouraged to believe that liberals want them to fund free services for all, and to believe that there was some focal point in the past in which they had everything they wanted, until immigrants and special interest groups took it all away. There is also an ongoing fear that liberals present an all-or-nothing proposition that is little more than a stepping-stone to a socialist state.

As a result, numerous issues have almost randomly identified as "conservative" and Republican: gun rights, the end to legalized abortion, the relaxation of environmental protection, the relaxation of industrial safety standards, the reduction of taxes, prayer in school, and the funding and support of the military. Conservative politicians and supporters associating and identifying themselves as Christians and patriots as long as they are friends of big business is nothing new. I see its genesis as 1980s Reaganomics. Reagan's view was that the ingredients of a strong America were strong economy, strong military, and strong families. Reagan did and does have many detractors and many supporters, both of him personally and of his performance as president. At the time of his election, he was viewed by liberals as conservative to the point of bigotry, and patriotic to the extent of hawkishness. Even at the time, however, most of his detractors were aware of his imposing physical presence, and his ability to communicate and deliver speeches clearly and effectively, both in person and to televised audiences. He was also by nature a quiet person in private, and he was not arrogant but had a long-standing confidence in his ability to talk to people, and that quality about him was something that I personally experienced soon after his election.

I was in New York during Ronald Reagan's first official visit to the city after his election, and I was invited to the reception being held in his honor. When he stood up to deliver a speech, which was being televised, I was very surprised to see he was using a teleprompter. This was not something I had ever seen a politician do, but of course Reagan's first profession was as an actor—and he was accustomed to approaching words and speaking in a studied professional capacity. The teleprompter allowed him to read a carefully worded speech while giving the appearance of someone speaking extemporaneously with ease.

My seat happened to be next to Marcus Wallenberg's, so we sat side by side listening to Reagan's speech. About ten minutes into the talk, Wallenberg turned to me and whispered: "This is great. He's like another Abraham Lincoln." I found it very interesting that he had this reaction, but I could also see where it came from. Reagan was doing an excellent job of looking, acting, and sounding presidential. It was, one might say, quite a performance. The teleprompter allowed him to do all this in a very relaxed, almost casual way, as if nothing could be easier than giving a statesman's speech. I have no recollection of what Reagan's speech was about, but I clearly remember how convincing its delivery was, just as I remember the admiration Marcus Wallenberg developed for Reagan by watching him talk. An accomplished public speaker and debater can make up for many other deficits, and certainly this was true for President Reagan.

Reagan was very clearly on the very conservative side of the American political system, and those who opposed him passionately did so with the genuine belief that he was bad for the country. But when it came to his foreign policy, and his interactions with foreign leaders whether approaching them as friend (Francois Mitterrand) or foe (Mikhail Gorbachev), Reagan affected a carefully cultivated heroic swagger—part cowboy and part general, where Jimmy Carter before him had been low-key and even lackluster in his personal affect with heads of state. Because of that charisma and confidence, even Reagan's detractors sometimes expressed admiration for the impression he made on foreign leaders. This is a quality that can be appreciated across party lines when international policy and America's global reputation are in the spotlight. One imagines feelings of acute embarrassment and shame across party lines when watching Trump interact with heads of state, though the GOP remain reluctant to admit even that much.

The European Union and the United States of America have often acted as checks and balances of sorts to one another, as allies with a common recent history and multiple common interests and markets. Throughout history, there has always been a rational basis for US/Europe cooperation and support. From Reagan to Bush, Clinton, and Obama, that US factor in that cooperation manifested in different ways, and in different levels, but the common thread was the spirit of cooperation itself, and the underlying commitment from which it came. So the EU was unprepared for the prospect of an American leader who places more value on soliciting the approval and friendship of the autocratic Russian leader Vladimir Putin than he does on any long-standing international ally.

Whatever impression Trump might give on television and in print, his first visit to Europe in 2017 gave an up close and personal confirmation to European leaders that their worst fears about the American president were more than justified. He insulted European leaders at every turn, while stirring up trouble in state politics whenever the opportunity presented itself. A *Financial Times* editorial at the time reported that, "It is now evident that Mr. Trump is not intent simply on defending American interests as he perceives them. Instead, he is actively intervening in European politics—to promote the agendas of nationalist parties that are his ideological soulmates."

The accounts of the presidential hubris on display both alarmed and pained many Americans. Trump's European counterpart is a study in contrasts—Germany's brilliant and enduring Angela Merkel—who is a real democrat and intellectual, has a passion for freedom, and is extremely useful in being an engine for the EU and a pillar of strength. It is almost beyond my ability to emotionally accept the possibility that fascism could prevail in France, or that Germany could return again to the dark. But adding the Trump insult to the existing injury of Brexit and growing fascist popularity in Europe gives rise to the possibility that the European Union could fail.

In a summer 2018 speech to the European Parliament, French President Emmanuel Macron said, "Indeed, in this world and this difficult moment, European democracy, I believe it very deeply, is our best chance. Faced with the authoritarianism that surrounds us everywhere, the answer is not an authoritarian democracy but the authority of democracy."

The United States has saved Europe in the past, but has otherwise shown little skill in dealing with South America, Africa, the Middle East, and Afghanistan, supporting the corrupt Saudi Arabia, and covering up their brutal mistakes in Vietnam. If the USA would now turn its back on the European Union, that would be a disastrous and historic mistake. In America and across the world, the natural impulse is still to feel as if someone will take action against the US president before letting things come to that. But as early as 2017, Trump publicly called the European Union an American foe, and in strictly political terms, there was virtually no American backlash. America's GOP has enjoyed something of a too-big-to-fail reputation for so long that even as the evidence of the Trump administration's incompetence and corruption began to pile up, the system remained in gridlock.

When it is tempting to see Trump's presidency as a departure from the norm that came out of the blue, we can look to the failure of another fabled, unsinkable institution—Wall Street. The financial collapse did not come out of the blue—on the contrary, as the years pass we continue to learn in more excruciating detail the long-term complicity of numerous organizations and agencies, in a cooperative venture of greed and self-interest in which money took precedence over the consumer, over shareholders, over investors, over the economy, over the law, and over even the most basic element of human decency.

For years preceding the financial crisis of 2008, Wall Street bankers were making huge investments lending money for domestic subprime mortgages. Wall Street's demand for buying, bundling, and reselling the subprime mortgages seemed to be insatiable, and in turn brokers grew more and more aggressive, awarding the loans to homeowners who were clearly underqualified and at high risk for default. Credit-rating agencies, designed to provide investors a trustworthy assessment of what was safe to buy, opted instead to issue top AAA ratings to the unsafe mortgage-backed securities in order to keep the Wall Street profits flowing. It was a cooperative venture in greed trumping all—the bankers knew, as did the regulators and the mortgage brokers, and the supervisory agency with the means and mandate of uncovering the true picture resorted instead to mass rubber-stamping. When no human stepped in to correct the institution, the scheme continued until housing prices reached their ultimate limit, upon which the entire structure imploded. As a result, countless people lost or were swindled out of their homes, or of investments that were rightfully theirs.

The banking collapse set off a series of chain reactions in which banks and financial institutions failed around the world.

It is remarkable that a bank can grow large and powerful over multiple generations, and still be vulnerable to shockwaves. In Switzerland, considered Europe's banking center, two major banks (Credit Suisse and UBS) were in danger of going under, as was the American giant Merrill Lynch, until their rescue by the Bank of America. But the cataclysm was no random act of God. Banks had operated without sufficient liquidity or had aggressively marketed extremely deceptive and flawed products in a sustained scam in which finance laws were repeatedly violated for years. How many of them were culpable? How many were punished? Each individual unethical cog in the corrupt machine could show they were just one of many bigger and more corrupt systems. The banks paid huge fees, but by and large, most of the human beings involved walked away from the whole mess.

And while it was tempting to scapegoat the Lehman Brothers bankruptcy as the inciting event, I know it is nowhere near that simple. In reality the entire US financial system was ethically bankrupt, and the fallout from that failing affected the entire world. When bank executives pocket almost $1.6 billion of taxpayer bailout money in salaries, bonuses, and benefits, with the average executive payout of $2.6 million—why did the shareholders then do nothing? The answer remains money—even after the extent of the disaster was realized, people were still lulled into passivity by the prospect of ending up with a little extra cash. This is endemic of a deeply serious problem in America, and as evident as the problems were in the aftermath of the financial crisis, the long-term effect on those at the top echelons of the banking world has been negligible.

The GOP's refusal to hold President Trump accountable for his catastrophic presidential performance is another manifestation of mass complicity and passivity that led up to and followed the financial crisis. And it is also motivated by money. In the wake of the banking crisis, the failure of an institution like Lehman Brothers was unthinkable—that was just the way it had to be, or the whole system would lose its presumptive infallibility. In the aftermath of the financial collapse, those who were still standing followed the impulse to dig in deeper, on the presumption that the prevailing public hostility toward the institution would pass, making it a worthwhile gamble to hang on to their spot. I think the same holds true for the GOP. When the GOP as a party looks at Trump, they can't see beyond the ramifications to the larger system of taking down one of their own. And on a human level, no one from a state senator to the house majority leader feels they can or must condemn President Trump because it seems like a better deal to gamble on either the survival of Trump or the survival of the GOP than to give up their seat at the table.

What does this mean for the future of the United States, and of the world? We can't look to the past for answers, because there is no precedent. We can't change the human propensity for corruption. But we also cannot change the Treaty of Rome, or the US Constitution. The US democracy has been strong enough in the past to carry the burden alone when Europe could not. The EU should be strong enough to carry the burden while America will not. But the possibility exists that they could both falter.

What will happen? The individual in charge will either succeed or fail. But the organization will still be standing unless its foundation is deliberately destroyed. The Constitution was designed to withstand times of growth and times of stagnancy, war and peace, and momentum toward the future as well as regression. There will always be another "unthinkable" scenario on the horizon. The political democratic system is at its core a transactional system, and one in which it is necessary to play the long game, to remember that long downward cycles have come before, and that institutions have endured. It is a system designed for adjustment and correction that, again, make it necessary to be in it for the long haul. If a leader has abandoned the principles and vision of the organization, that organization can still be returned to its core principles later on. The Constitution and the Treaty of Rome are indestructible.

So what must we do? There is one thing—we must accept a lesson when presented with it and use what we have learned to better assess and elect the next person to be in charge. Some will be great, some tepid, some in the middle. While the driver may prove unpredictable, the car is anything but. It is designed with backup systems and safety systems that enable it to endure and to keep going, getting us where we want to be so that the next person we put behind the wheel knows where we need to go, and how to get there.

EPILOGUE

Epilogue. *French epilogue, < Latin epilogus, < Greek* ἐπίλογος *the peroration of a speech, <* ἐπί *in addition +* λόγος, *speech. A summary.*
The concluding part of a literary work; an appendix.
—Oxford English Dictionary

I originally intended this epilogue to provide a summary of my view of the world today, and of my most significant experiences in it—the crowning overview of a book that had its genesis in my inclination to write a memoir. I've never been particularly interested in myself as the subject of anything—and while I have many remarkable stories about people I've known and places to which I've been, I nonetheless find that at the age of eighty-four, I am still at best ambivalent about the appeal of my personal narrative, which is after all, what a memoir is. So I suppose it is not surprising that in the process of working on this book, I discovered that what I really wanted to write was not the Pehr Gyllenhammar story, but rather the stories of Pehr Gyllenhammar.

This seems fitting, as I have often thought my life has been something of a roller-coaster ride. As such, I am a person best seen through a connection of episodes and anecdotes—and while

I have never much enjoyed talking about my personal life, I do find it fascinating to talk about the company of good people that I have loved. I have always felt that friendships and family are the most vital elements of the human experience. It is from colleagues, friends, and family that I have learned the most important lessons, and my connections to people—whether at work, at home, or in my travels throughout the world—are what allowed me to exceed the abilities and capacities with which I was born, and to become a person who, I believe, has been of value in the world. Of course, there cannot be connection without disconnection. Not all relationships remain fruitful over the long haul. In the world of business, jobs come and go. Friends and associates come and go. In the end, particularly if we are lucky enough to run the full course of a long life, what gives it meaning and purpose is not the jobs, or the battles won, or the prizes or accolades accrued. The meaning comes from the core of our human connections, especially those closest to us. In all of my relationships, from professional to personal, I think I have been wise in my choices, and profoundly lucky in terms of meeting the right people at the right time. If I had it to do all over again, there is not much I would change. There are very few things I regret in my life—maybe that is hubris, but that is the person I am.

My view of the state of the world in these pages has often been dark—some might call it a pessimism fueled by fear that the dream of an enlightened and humanistic world has all but—to my eyes—disappeared. It is not always easy for me to embrace optimism about the future when something so crucial and precious—humanistic integrity—is so scarce. That scarcity gives a sense of impermanence and murkiness to life—one is always wondering if it is gone for good, leaving us in a waking nightmare where the beauty that sustained us has faded—as the poet Keats put it, "Fled is that music:—Do I wake or sleep?"

I have talked at some length about the present prospects of the United States and the European Union. Significant developments arise so rapidly it is hard to get one's bearings. No sooner is the ink dry on one astonishing headline of a newspaper than the next, even more astonishing headline is already churning off the presses or pulsing across the internet at light speed. There are complex currents and eddies at work on every continent. At this time in Europe, the prevailing parties in Poland (Law and Justice) and in Hungary (Viktor Orbán's Fidesz party) have become authoritarian to the point where the EU have issued them warnings. Austria and Italy have shown strong neo-Nazi tendencies. Russia, which bridges the continents of Europe and Asia, is in the throes of a brutal dictatorship, and struggles with an unaffordable military and a dismal economy.

But in Asia, there have been some surprising gains. India is grown into a wonderful democracy—the biggest in the world. Tiny Singapore has proven to be a good model for survival under "firm leadership." And while China is under a harsh dictatorship (not unlike Mao's), their rate of growth and the amount of power they now wield is amazing. Asia is extraordinary in its diversity and strength. In the far west of the continent, the nations comprising the Middle East region are tragically hobbled by continuing armed conflicts under cruel dictators whose brutality seems to have no limits.

Africa has great promise, with a manifold group of countries and resources. Drought and starvation continue to be one of the continent's most challenging problems. Australia is unique in being a very large island comprised by a single nation, and as a whole it is comfortable and rich in natural resources. In South

America there is a mixture of corruption and fascist tendencies and the continent as a whole is experiencing a decline in growth and discipline, which makes for a troubling situation.

From my own experience, I feel the most crucial issues at hand can be condensed into just a few institutions or systems which must be defended, rescued, and revitalized at all costs. The first, of course, is democracy in the purest and most humanistic sense. Another is the environmental health of the planet, and the fight to begin turning the tide of global warming. The third is the state of the global media, and the preservation of the ability of major media organizations to survive as independent, integrity-centered institutions.

In truth, it seems increasingly obvious that the future of both democracy and the geo-climate are predicated on the existence of an honest and fair media. News has become commoditized, and in the interest of making a profit it is common practice to put a charlatan on the news and label him an "expert." The so-called expert can spout whatever nonsense they please, and it is presented as legitimate, which completely undermines the integrity of the media outlet. Many of the fairly good publications throughout the Western world are now gone, and the media is in the ether. In the United States there are still news sources that remain credible like the *New York Times*, *Washington Post*, *Los Angeles Times*, and the *Chicago Tribune*, but the prevailing trend is the multimedia, which is essentially noise from everywhere and much less reliable than the traditional media.

If I had to reduce all of this decline to a single source, I would say it is a widespread lack of ethos. Without it, we will continue to spin out of control. The Greek root of the word "ethos" means the house you build. Morality, on the other hand, is grounded in communal mores—the law of the tribe. So while morality is received—ethos is made or built. Both are constantly under siege by the Machiavellian triad of money/fame/power. In many nations today, Machiavelli is coming out on top.

My views and projections of the future for these many nations have and will continue to evolve greatly over the decades. The same is true in terms of my feelings about my native country of Sweden. Not all of my views on that subject are popular ones. I am one of a minority who think, for example, that we can and should get rid of the Swedish monarchy. They hold no political power anymore, and in the twenty-first century they have become primarily a function of ceremony and decoration. Monarchical supporters would argue that the monarchy cannot do any harm because they have no political power, and that is true, making it somewhat hard to defend my point that we should dispense with them. But my dislike of them is not simply because they are lame ducks. I think the British monarchy is actually a good model for what that system can do, and how it can best coexist with government. My real problem with the Swedish royal family is that they have Nazi roots. It was recently exposed that the father of Queen Silvia (who is German) was a Nazi who enriched himself by seizing a Jewish armaments factory in 1939, taking over its operations and pocketing all of the profits. Certain members of the royal family were unapologetic after this revelation—the queen's brother called it an outright lie. It is, unfortunately, very true, and is one of the major reasons I have this negative opinion of the royal family, an opinion I have publicly shared. As a result, the royal family probably has a pretty negative opinion of me too, with good reason.

There was a time I couldn't have imagined that I would ever have any feelings that could be construed as anti-Swedish. But as I have previously stated in this book, the seeds of my discomfort with my country were planted in my childhood as a direct result of Sweden's accommodation of the Nazis during the Second World War. To my thinking, it was at that time that the character of the Swedish nation became something my ancestor Mans Andersson would not have recognized. I've shared my theory that when Sweden chose Bernadotte as their crown prince in the nineteenth century, it marked the moment when the nation began to move in the wrong direction, and the national characteristics of probity and conviction that Mans Andersson espoused began to change. I would now add that Sweden's conduct in World War II cemented the new national character in place. Bernadotte was the turning point, but after the war, there was no turning back.

I feel it important to separate my feelings about Sweden-the-nation from my feelings about the Swedish people. For whatever reasons, I have been looked up to as a role model by many people in my country, and that is not something that I take lightly. Hemingway wrote that Paris is a moveable feast—someone who has known that place and lived side by side with Parisians will carry it with them for the rest of their life. I think this holds true for the many things I loved about Sweden—especially the factory workers at Volvo. I think the best aspects of a place we have known for any time as home do stay with us long after we have moved on, particularly if we have worked to achieve some communal good while living there. I have lived in cities such as Gothenburg, New York, and London, and in any place I have called home, I have tried to support and facilitate youth activities, crime prevention agencies, and the arts. Music and the availability to the public of high-quality musical performances has been something in particular that I've tried to facilitate, both financially and in serving on boards and using whatever influence and networks I have to be of benefit to organizations such as the Gothenburg Symphony Orchestra and the London Philharmonic Orchestra.

I think my affinity for music (in my case as a supporter, not a performer) is directly related to the fact that my mother was a pianist. I've found that often it is our own families (and involvement of specific family members) who bring us the inclination and opportunity to engage and work to effect change on a local level, in regional organizations. By way of an example, in Sweden back in the 1970s both of my daughters were riders. I found much fault with the equestrian environment, particularly for girls. I was upset by way the horses were treated, and by the male supremacy that prevailed in everything from class management to stable maintenance. I found the whole atmosphere to be very anti-feminist. As a result (and making a long story short) I started my own riding organization in Gothenburg and featured a horse show that became the first international equestrian competition. The organization I created naturally reflected my own values and opinions about how female equestrians should (and should not) be treated, resulting in a much friendlier environment for my daughters and for all girls and women. My involvement in the equestrian world waned as my daughters grew older and eventually stopped riding, but it's an accomplishment that I'm still proud of today.

I'm in no way implying that my greatest pleasures in life have all come from altruism, nor am I the kind of person who eschews enjoying some of the money I have worked hard to earn. I have never sought to emulate the kind of zero-sum philanthropy of someone like Andrew Carnegie, for whom "winning" ultimately meant giving everything away (which included providing for his dependents). My worldly successes have afforded me the opportunity to indulge in some interests and hobbies that are not universally practical. One of them is sailing. I was never particularly interested in the more passive manifestations of the activity (often collective termed "cruising"). What I was extremely interested in doing was racing, specifically in racing keelboats of the Dragon class, a design well loved for its long keel and sleek lines, and which was the 1929 brainchild of the Norwegian sailor and yacht designer Johan Anker. In my Dragon *Amanda* (often with my dear friend and navigator Niclas Granberg) I competed in some of the most notorious and grueling courses in the world, including the Cowes Race in the Solent around the Isle of Wight, during which we survived a violent hurricane and were among the sixty boats to ultimately complete the course, out of the 600 that began the course that day. We won the race.

I've also been fortunate to be able to indulge in my passion for collecting French wines, an interest that—like sailing—I probably inherited from my father. The oldest bottle currently in my collection is an 1899 Chateau d'Yquem, a sweet wine that has the distinction of being the only Sauternes wine in the Bordeaux classification to have been giving the rating of 1st Cru Classé Supérieur. The appreciation of such a wine must be experienced firsthand so I won't try to describe it, but in a Sotheby's sale catalog of an 1899 Chateau d'Yquem, a sip of this vintage was described as resembling "the silence that follows a piece by Mozart, in which the listener remains suffused with the music."

My interest in wine extends to the history of the Official Wine Classification of 1855, which is still in use today. The classification was ordered by Napoleon, with all wines ranked to reflect their quality, so that only the Bordeaux region's finest wines would be featured at the Exposition Universelle de Paris. France is the only country in the world where they have this kind of extremely strict classification discipline. No one else in world has it or has tried to copy it, because it is difficult to comply. There are many regulations, such as vines should always be naturally grown (resulting in bad years when climate is rough), and it is forbidden to irrigate any vineyard—failure to comply means being closed out of the classification system (a disgrace of almost incalculable proportions in Bordeaux). The system ranks by growth or cut of the crop, with the first cut, Premier Crus, being the highest. Only four estates made the Premier Crus ranking in that 1855 classification: Chateau Lafite Rothschild, Pauillac; Chateau Latour, Pauillac; Chateau Margaux, Margaux; and Chateau Haut-Brion, Graves (since 1986, Pessac-Leognan).

It may be that my enthusiasm for the classification of wine is because its precision is so nonlinear. An oenophile does not simply like a certain kind of wine year after year, since quality is never consistent. Sequential history in wine is of no importance—classification derives precision by using a regional appellation, a quality designation, and a year. I find this a fitting symbol for the way in which I look back at my life now—not in a single, continuous line but in individual episodes I can identify by a certain year and a certain person or place. As such, my perspective of the past is akin to seeing a mountainous landscape from a great height—a range of varied peaks—some close, and some far in the distance, which draw the eye and attention, leaving unseen the valleys and gullies below that connect each mountain to the next. That is how I like to look at my life, and so I have given an impressionist's view of it in these pages, where people and places come into view, and when perceived as a whole it is my hope that readers will see a life that comes into focus.

Because I have written about my life in this way, there will inevitably be omissions of people and places that are of no less importance than those included in this book, but simply happen to be parts of the story that I did not tell this time around. I don't consider myself to be an expert in the art of narrative, but I do know that a good storyteller always remembers to save a few tales for another day. I also know that this epilogue—which began with my taking a broad look at the developments on the major continents in the world—should find resolution in something occupying a much smaller scale in size—my family.

I was married to Christina Engellau Gyllenhammar for forty-nine years—she was my life partner from 1959 until the day she died in September of 2008. As a widower at the age of seventy-three, I fully expected that a certain chapter in my life had ended. My children Cecilia, Charlotte, Oscar, and Sophie were fully grown and had each found their own path as adults. I had grandchildren to enjoy, with every expectation there would be more on the way. I did not feel I needed anything that life had not already given me—I only knew that I had no intention of cutting back on my work schedule, or on the international travel that went with it. I kept myself moving. And for that reason, there came a day when I found myself on a flight from London to Copenhagen sitting next to a lovely woman who I could see was much younger than I was. Just a few minutes into conversation, I realized she was also one of the most intelligent people I'd ever spoken to. And I've spoken to a lot of people.

Lee Welton Croll, I soon learned, was a British-Canadian with a PHD in Industrial & Organizational Psychology, as well as a licensed and chartered occupational psychologist. As we sat on the plane chatting, I quickly found myself immersed in an in-depth discussion about the state of the European Union. Beyond being highly educated, I could see that Lee was extraordinarily well informed. In disagreement with me about some now forgotten theoretic statement I had made about the restructuring of the European Rust Belt, she countered my position with the mathematical precision of a geometrician—her customary approach in any discourse—which is highly analytical, factually supported, and paving the way with axioms, postulates, and proven facts before arriving at her concluding point.

I was absolutely captivated.

Lee and I were married on April 19, 2013. The Swedish media followed the event closely, in articles that were occasionally celebratory, but sometimes pointlessly mean-spirited in the long-standing tabloid tradition of unpleasantness. The *Göteborgs-Posten* headline simply read "Newly Wed: Pehr G. Gyllenhammar," while the *Expressen* opted for dubious specificity with the headline "PG's 38 Year Younger Wife: Kallat's Gold Digger." I was not surprised, but nonetheless I was deeply disappointed, and hurt on Lee's behalf. The Swedish press seemed to underestimate my new wife in virtually every way possible. Nonetheless, I was unwilling to allow the press to detract from my own happiness at having found someone who was so perfectly matched with me, both intellectually and personally. It was almost unreasonable to think that life had anything more with which to gift me. But I was wrong about that.

On January of 2016, our daughter Barrett was born. To find myself a father at the age of eighty was beyond delightful, and a new level of energy and purpose cascaded into my life. I cannot imagine my life without Lee or Barrett—they are among the most important and essential elements of my world. When two people who enjoy having conversations about global politics have a child together, those conversations of necessitude begin to include the presence of that child. Lee has said to me on more than one occasion, "Where on earth will Barrett be able to live when she's grown up? What will she be able to eat and drink when we have microplastics at every level of the food chain and shrinking sources of clean potable water?" She cites the mass displacement of population that will occur if predictions are right about rising sea levels and temperatures, and the gap between the haves and the have-nots that is likely to increase with the rise of artificial intelligence that will only exacerbate things. Where will Barrett fit into this chaotic future?

We talk about what we can do now, in the moment, to help our daughter prepare for a future that is imbued with a great deal of uncertainty. Certainly one thing people will have to be in the future is very financially savvy. As someone whose field of expertise involves a comprehensive understanding of both work and workers, Lee knows it's going to be harder and harder for people to earn a living. She also predicts that in the future basic skills are going to be in short supply for a lot of people, because of all the specific, narrow skill sets that will be required of people in the coming decades.

Recently we had a conversation about higher education, and the kind of education on all levels that will be the most important for Barrett to acquire. Lee believes, quite rightly in my opinion, that the key value of higher education is not the content of that education, but rather in teaching young people *how* to learn and think, not *what* to think. As she put it, "I think it's really essential that you don't just teach people a trade or a skill or a vocation and give them content knowledge for a job—but that you also teach them the ability to think critically and analytically, so that they are able to clearly communicate ideas and present an argument logically and compellingly. And in many jobs, people will need to have the ability to handle large volumes of data, to be able to sift through it and make decisions about what is relevant and what is important as opposed to what is just noise in the system."

A great many decisions lie ahead of us during the years in which we are guiding our daughter into adulthood. One decision on which we both immediately agreed was about where we wanted or did not want to raise our child. With our combined passports, the choices are Sweden, England, Canada, and the United States. We have both been emphatic on one point: we do not want to raise our child in the United States. And yet in the not too distant past, we would both have had the opposite feeling. Lee told me that "even ten years ago I would have regarded it as a golden ticket to have a US passport to be an American citizen—in the country where anything was possible. But now I'm not convinced that her US citizenship is going to be such a blessing for her in the long run."

My feelings about the US have grown considerably darker. Lee will correct me when I use the word "evil," but certainly the country has come into the clutches of some evil people. I have in past years been a great admirer of the US Constitution and the flexibility and broadness that characterizes it, but Trump has capitalized on that broadness and manipulated it to a stunning degree to both circumvent the law and the principles of the Constitution itself. For that reason, I now see how brittle the Constitution is and how much potential for danger it has, both through what the current president is doing, and the fact that in the future another president could manipulate it again.

In addition to questions of where to live and how to live, Lee and I frequently talk about the kind of person we hope Barrett will become. We both want Barrett to grow up to be a person with empathy and compassion for others, and we would hope that she would not get pulled into the egocentric focus that seems to be fairly widespread now among young people due to the prevalence of social media. We hope that she will have a sense of personal accountability and responsibility for shaping her own choices and the world she lives in, and for not putting herself at the center of everything that she does.

In our lives and in our work, Lee and I have both tried to serve others and to make whatever contribution we can to help people—whether individually or in their communities and workplaces—to be happier and healthier. I am hopeful that Barrett will emulate that quality as well. I think we both would be terribly disappointed if our daughter were to grow up as a myopic, self-focused, or entitled person.

Recently, Lee and I discussed Barrett's future at length, as we contemplated making a move from our London home. As always, Lee was both passionate and clear about what she felt it most important for Barrett to learn. She said, "You have to stand up and take risks, and be willing to put your neck on the line for a truly important principle—you can't afford to be silent. People need to know when the time is right to come together and act. That's something you've always had, Pehr, a sense of agency and a real desire to take action in order to improve things. If Barrett and even a percentage of her peers have those qualities like empathy, fortitude, and courage fostered and encouraged in their childhoods, they'll grow into adults who have the means and the character to bring about the kind of significant change that the world is really going to need."

I can only conclude by saying that I've had a great deal of excellent luck in my life, and meeting Lee, and parenting a young child with a woman of this caliber is quite possibly the greatest stroke of luck of all. More than ever, I'm aware of how much I really have that is of value. In my eighth decade, I have a healthy and enduring family—grown children and growing grandchildren, as well as the continuing friendship of some truly great human beings who are still, for better or worse, alive and in this world. Many more among those family and friends are long gone, and now only memories—but the loss of their physical presence has never diminished their effect on me, nor diminished the strength I derive from them.

I have worked hard and well, and from those times when my work has been rewarding, the pride and happiness in what I've achieved has remained with me always. Much of my experience has been on the large scale, and what makes for big victories makes also for big losses. I find nothing whatsoever to be ashamed of in the fact that as a substantial person, I have experienced some substantial failures. I'm not proud of my failures, but I am proud of the way that I handled them.

A life lived consistently will bring consistent results. I've often been single-minded and uncompromising in my insistence that things be done right, and that they be done truthfully, and that they be done fairly. Early on in life I began to identify myself as a humanist, and I have never stopped seeing and appreciating the value and importance of human beings. And the result of my efforts, both successful and unsuccessful, to make my vision of humanism a reality has been the consistent appearance of people in my life who espouse the very qualities that I so earnestly wish upon the world as a whole.

There are other areas in which I have not been so focused and single-minded, and we can include those in the file marked "Stories for Another Book." For the time being, the story ends here: My wife walks into the room holding Barrett, whose arms are entwined around her mother's neck. As I watch them, I think of how many people in the world have, in varying ways, paved the way for this moment in a web of connectives that stretches centuries into the past. In my mind's eye, I can see no farther back than an arbitrary moment I consider the past-beginning—when a farmer named Andersson was asked to stand up for Sweden and to join the fight for king and crown. And with my own eyes—in the bright and sweet faces of my wife and child—I can see the moment I think of as the future-beginning. It is this moment. It is these people. It is now.

AFTERWORD
by Dr. Lee Croll

Many books and articles have been written about my husband Pehr, in an attempt to identify and better understand the unique features and personal attributes that have allowed him to achieve such a high level of accomplishment and success over the course of his life. When asked directly about the drivers and characteristics that underpin his many achievements, Pehr's answers tend to be minimal and terse. He is not one to regularly or naturally engage in deep self-reflection. As such, these types of questions are generally not of much interest to Pehr and, at times, they can generate more pique and annoyance than insight. By his nature he is a very present and future-oriented person. As someone who is privileged to know him well (and who coincidentally holds a PhD in Industrial & Organizational Psychology), I'm often asked for insights into his personality and character. I find that people are especially interested in understanding the qualities in Pehr that draw people to him and enable him to be such an effective and sought out leader. There is no simple answer to this, given the complex interactions between personality, competencies and situational/contextual factors. However, over the years I've had ample opportunity to develop insights into his leadership style and personal attributes.

It is a well-established fact in the field of I/O Psychology that General Intelligence is the sine qua non of success in the executive suite. However, intelligence, in and of itself, does not guarantee followership (the core essence of leadership) or inspire trust and commitment on the part of employees and organizational stakeholders. Pehr is, of course, highly intelligent. However, in order to explain the deep loyalty, respect, and high esteem that so many have for Pehr, a more robust and nuanced explanation is required.

I have spent the last 20 years assessing senior executives across a wide variety of industries and in my experience, great leadership can only be achieved when intelligence is complemented by strong interpersonal skills, drive, integrity, and the ability to define and articulate a compelling vision for the organization. It is in this regard that Pehr's exceptionalism shines through. He displays a unique blend of intelligence, charisma, integrity, and determination. There can even appear to be something almost intangible and instinctual about his leadership approach.

Without a doubt he is charismatic. When he walks into a room of people, heads turn, and without even intending to, he naturally commands attention. And while Pehr does not actively seek out the spotlight, I believe that once in it, he finds the attention and affirmation enjoyable and invigorating. Much has been made of the charismatic leader—both good and bad—in the press and in management theory. For decades now we have lived in a world of celebrity CEOs and a cult of personality has allowed numerous lackluster talents to succeed in the upper echelons of business via impression management. Thankfully, irrespective of their charisma, unless an individual also possesses considerable substance and competence they rarely hold up over time as a CEO and they often leave a brittle legacy. It is undeniable that over the course of Pehr's career, there have been professional highs and lows. However, despite these peaks and troughs, it is indisputable that both he and his legacy have withstood the test of time. Of course this kind of long term primacy cannot exist without creating its share of dissenters, but his legacy remains—as evidenced last year by being named number one in Sweden in a poll about the country's best leaders (notably nearly twenty-five years after leaving Volvo).

As a starting point, I think it is important to differentiate between the terms charm and charisma, even though the terms are often used interchangeably in everyday life. In my experience, charm is frequently a form a manipulation, a "tell" that the individual may have a hidden agenda or concealed motives. It is a characteristic that, as a psychologist, I am always wary of—especially when conducting executive assessments. Charisma, in contrast, is a more value-neutral attribute. It is a manifestation of a more elemental magnetism; the ability to draw people towards you and your ideas without it necessarily being intentional or a function of a hidden agenda. In light of this distinction, I regard Pehr through my professional lens as someone who is charismatic but not charming. With him, what you see is what you get—and what you get is often very compelling. However, he is too direct, honest and blunt—sometimes verging on abrasive—to be considered a masterful charmer. As such, despite his magnetism, he continues to have rough edges.

I personally think that it is a combination of his charisma and his deep sense of integrity that afford him such a powerful interpersonal impact. People want to talk to him and to hear what he has to say. And the fact that his values are readily apparent—both in his words and actions—gives credibility and weight to what he says. Further, looking at Pehr's time as Volvo's CEO, the attributes that set him apart were his insight and vision, his directness and reputation for absolute honesty, and his rock-solid commitment to innovation and humanism in the workplace. At Volvo, his stated principles and intentions were consistently followed by actions that bore those intentions out. This trustworthiness and steadfast commitment to humanistic values engendered great loyalty, which, in all but the highest levels of management, was nearly universal among the company's employees.

Through my work in executive assessment over the last 20 years, I have observed that courageousness, determination, and values-based leadership can sometimes be threatening to a small yet powerful subset of people within an organization. Typically, one finds these types of people in mid and upper management positions, though their span of influence is greatest when they are in or just below the C-suite. Managers and executives who fit this profile generally prefer to jockey for position and advance their careers through politicking and sycophancy, rather than actual talent or hard work. Unfortunately, these individuals often take steps to undermine their most transparent and talented colleagues—such as leaders like Pehr—since they regard them as incorruptible and therefore uncontrollable. Given how often I have seen this dynamic occur, it would not be unreasonable to speculate that it was likely at play during Pehr's time at Volvo. That said, irrespective of the politics during his final years at Volvo, the loyalty and influence Pehr built up as CEO was exceptional. It was unique to him, and never equaled by his successors.

Arguably, Pehr's leadership has had an impact far beyond Volvo. One can reasonably assert that he is a cultural icon within Sweden and the larger Nordic area. He and I have spent much of the last eight years in Stockholm and it is not an exaggeration to say that almost every time we go out multiple people come up to him, asking to shake his hand and saying things like, "thank you for everything you've done for this country—you are my hero" or "you have influenced my professional choices and inspired me to achieve". Pehr tends to discount this kind of spontaneous, positive feedback by saying that people are simply being nice. However, it is obvious to me that these are people who have genuinely been impacted by him, since, as a rule of thumb, people do not generally go out of their way to offer praise and compliments to strangers.

It is clear to me that Pehr has impacted and inspired people from all walks of life. Generally, it is the feedback that he has received from working class people that he has found the most touching and meaningful. It comes as little surprise to me that Pehr has often been quoted as saying that, in business, the people he likes best are the workers. And I suspect that fact was evident to his employees at Volvo as well. The visits he regularly made to the factory floor exemplify some of the qualities that set him apart from other corporate leaders of the time. Unlike today's typically flat and matrixed organizations, companies at the time were very much a top down, command-and-control structure. Factory workers rarely saw or interacted with their company's CEO and it is unlikely that many would even recognize their CEO if he passed them in the hallway. The power differential was significant—there was a huge gulf between the revered chief executive and the fungible worker who was generally regarded as little more than a cog in the machine. By making the effort to physically show up on the shop floor and talk to—and listen to—the workers, Pehr upended conventional management thought and practice, replacing it with something significantly more forward looking and modern. Unlike today, when many leaders engage in corporate walkabouts as a means of damage control, this was not an exercise in optics. Pehr was genuinely interested in his workers' input and in understanding their experience of the workplace. By giving thought to the nature of their work and creating a mechanism for workers to give voice to their opinions, ideas and frustrations, Pehr created a bi-directional channel of communication that fundamentally altered the power dynamic within the company as well as how the work itself was performed. By flouting conventional organizational structure and process, he was able to achieve considerable competitive advantage. But more importantly, at its most fundamental level, doing so showed his respect for the workers and reinforced their dignity and worth as people.

North Americans often ask me if Pehr's leadership style reflects a typical Swedish approach or ethos, particularly as the country has positioned itself as a beacon of progressive values, design and innovation. But by most measures, Pehr is not a conventional Swede, not just in terms of his approach to business but also in his everyday life. To better provide insight into him for a North American audience, I would offer a few contextual and illustrative observations that I made over the course of the time we spent together in Sweden. As background, I come from an international upbringing—I hold passports from three different countries, and I have had the good fortune of living and working in many of the greatest and most dynamic cities around the world. As such, I am no stranger to expat life and the challenges that foreigners face when attempting to integrate into other cultures and societies.

Before my life with Pehr, my impression of Sweden was that it was a very liberal, open, and tolerant country, with a decidedly modern embrace of issues like gay marriage, access to education and universal healthcare. Although much of this is true, I was surprised by the extent to which certain aspects of everyday life in Stockholm were relatively rigid and conventional. Obviously there are always exceptions, but I was frequently struck by the degree of uniformity when it came to dress as well as the high levels of consistency across people's views and behavior. And it quickly became apparent that even small deviations from the socially proscribed way of doing things would result in obvious discomfort and/or embarrassment on the part of others or, worse still, swift censure of the transgressor.

As an anecdotal example of this, I remember an amusing incident once when we attended the birthday of one of Pehr's grandchildren in Stockholm. The party was intended to be an informal event, scheduled on a weekend afternoon at the parents' house. The guest list was comprised of a few family members and half a dozen children. As such, I was surprised when Pehr put on a suit and tie, and I pointed out that he seemed a little overdressed for a nine-year-old's party.

"All the men will be wearing suits and ties," Pehr said. "If someone shows up without a tie the other men will be uncomfortable, and they won't know what to do."

I had trouble believing this was truly the case, so Pehr decided to conduct a little experiment. He would go to the party wearing a suit, but without a tie, he told me.

"Watch and see what happens," he said.

And, indeed, when we arrived all the men had on suits and ties. However, within 20 minutes of my tie-less husband's arrival, every other man there had subtly removed their own tie. I found the results of that experiment very telling and, although I do not profess to have cracked the Swedish psyche, at the time, it offered an important insight into the subtle ways in which Swedes can be attached to convention and conformity.

Consequently, one of the ways in which I consider Pehr a somewhat "atypical" Swede is his lack of conventionality and conformity. Throughout his entire life he has walked his own path, often taking the road less travelled. As a leader, he has been outspoken about what he thought was best, be it for Volvo, Sweden, or Europe—even when it was unpopular or to his detriment. He is resolute in his commitment to ideas, principles, and humanistic values. His independence of mind and spirit have allowed him to take courageous, stand-alone decisions—both as a leader and as an individual—even in the face of public criticism and opposition. He is outspoken and opinionated, rarely shying away from a challenge or debate. Of course, as a result of these attributes, some people can experience him as irascible and cantankerous. However, irrespective of his sometimes prickly temper, most people appreciate the fact that he is straightforward, direct and honest. They know that, with Pehr, there are no games or hidden agendas. Although at times he may cause offence, it is never through malice and one can trust that he is sincere in what he says.

One might worry that this constellation of personal attributes paired with such a commanding presence could lead him to be overbearing and self-important. Perhaps some people regard him as such. However, in my experience with Pehr this is not the case. What enables him to be a dominant alpha type without being domineering, per se, is the fact that Pehr is broad-minded and genuinely does not view himself as superior to others. He regards no one as being above or below him, from the highest echelons of business and government to the shop floor worker and support staff. As a consequence, Pehr has won the respect of and enjoyed lasting friendships with many of the world's most talented leaders and thinkers. Moreover, he has also been able to build lasting loyalty and respect among the former front-line staff who worked for him.

Although Pehr is orderly, he is not rigid. Rather, he tends to be a lateral, conceptual thinker who has limited interest in extraneous detail. He is curious, broad-minded, and open to new experiences. In this regard, his problem-solving style diverges from one of the more prevalent approaches I encountered while in Sweden, which emphasized the importance of adhering closely to established, customary ways of doing things. By way of example, I frequently found that in Sweden relatively banal queries and requests were met with a flat "No, that cannot be done here. In Sweden we do things this way…". Whether intended or not, this type of response often implied a degree of inflexibility and conventionalism. Further, to a non-Swede it could often come across as patronizing or disdainful of other customs and practices, as though implying that Sweden had all the "right" answers. Once when discussing this phenomenon with a well-travelled and internationally-minded Swedish friend, he jokingly offered by way of explanation that this type of response was because his compatriots "could only think in straight lines, never around corners". Although I'm not sure that I would go that far in my assessment of Swedes, the frequency with which I was confronted by this type of response was astonishing.

Through my experience of everyday life in Stockholm, it quickly became evident that subtle rules of convention applied to a great many aspects of one's life, more so than anywhere else that I have lived. To my chagrin, I frequently encountered judgement and disapproval on issues ranging from the banal (e.g., choosing to decorate our flat using a strong color palette in eggshell finish instead of the more ubiquitously used matte white paint) to far more important ones, such as my "right" to have a child with my husband, a decision which provoked all sorts of sanctimonious debate and criticism, given our respective ages.

For all of Sweden's emphasis on egalitarianism and openness, I was surprised to encounter vestiges of elitism and nationalism as frequently as I did. A not insignificant subset of the people I interacted with placed considerable importance on social class and Swedish heritage. To my dismay, I was often reminded of my "outsider" status and made to feel not particularly welcome—an experience I discovered was not uncommon among the expats I knew in Stockholm—despite being a polite, educated professional from a similar cultural background who was married to a well-respected Swede. On more than one occasion I was told that I should "go back where I came from" and "what a loss for you that you are not Swedish". Although the class system may not be as overt as it is in some countries, there were still subtle ways in which status was signaled. For example, many people in Sweden expressed surprise and consternation when I chose not to take my husband's last name after we were married, frequently making comments to me such as "Why would you not take Gyllenhammar as your last name? It would show others that you are nobility!".

In light of this, when reflecting on Pehr's time at Volvo, I find it striking that a CEO, let alone one from a wealthy, well-known, ennobled family, would take such a strong interest in his shop floor workers, treating them with a level of respect and courtesy typically reserved for those in more powerful positions within the organization. I can imagine how that the lack of elitism in Pehr's leadership engendered considerable loyalty, appreciation, and commitment among his workers and those who shared a humanistic orientation. Conversely, I do not think that it would be an overreach to assume that Pehr's refusal to adhere to convention and society's hierarchical norms might have generated resentment among some in positions of power who would have preferred that he preserve the status quo—both in business and the broader society. Anecdotally, it always struck me that the people who were most effusive in their praise and appeared to appreciate and respect Pehr the most were often those in the trenches and frontlines of business, specifically the working and middle classes. In comparison, many members of the social and business "elite" demonstrated greater ambivalence, often seeking to engage with Pehr publicly while simultaneously revealing a degree of resentment and envy towards him.

Pehr is well known for the grand scale of his vision and for his pursuit of objectives that others might deem impossible. He is a visionary who has often sought to drive transformative change in the organization he is leading. He is unperturbed by seemingly insurmountable challenges and obstacles, trusting that there is always a way forward if the strategic course is set correctly. Historically, some have been skeptical, if not critical, of his ideas, such as the Norway Deal. However, with time and the luxury of hindsight one can see that his ambitions were rarely misplaced.

Courageous leadership is not for those with a weak ego and, over the years, much has been made of Pehr's charisma and the extent to which that characteristic can often bleed into narcissism. To be clear, we are all narcissistic to some extent, none of us are completely free from ego. Further, self-belief and a strong sense of personal agency are both critical to success and advancement within a business context. Thus, when assessing executives, the more relevant issue becomes the extent to which a person's narcissism is productive or unproductive (or worse, pathological). The "bright side" of narcissistic leaders is their charisma and larger than life persona, strong strategic thinking skills, big-picture focus, comfort with risk and uncertainty, self-belief, and the ability to influence others and build enthusiasm around a shared set of goals. If one thinks about it, of course it takes some degree of narcissism to be willing (and able) to drive massive transformation—without it few would have the audacity to even try. Where narcissism becomes unproductive and toxic in an organizational setting is when attributes such as grandiosity, self-promotion, lack of empathy/ exploitation of others, unwillingness to hear alternative points of view and prioritization of one's own personal gain are key drivers. Despite whatever hubris he may display, Pehr demonstrates all the bright side attributes with a limited dark side "shadow". Had it been otherwise, his legacy could not have endured, and his star would have been extinguished long ago.

Pehr has always driven hard for the objectives he believed were strategically important, rarely being put off by barriers or obstacles. He has done so throughout his career knowing full well that his determination might not sit well with some of his fellow executives. Independence of mind paired with tenacity rarely come without a cost, and for Pehr it has led to some significant clashes. One aspect of conflict management that I believe he still grapples with is determining which of the proverbial hills he is prepared to die on, especially when battling other corporate goliaths. Because his decisions are so deeply rooted in his personal values and principles, he has the inclination to fight every battle to the very end, even when doing so might ultimately be to his detriment. Needless to say, interpersonal politics and organizational turf wars are of little interest to Pehr and he is not particularly adept at navigating them. Fortunately, he operates at a sufficiently senior level that these dynamics are less pervasive. However, when they do come into play, there can be fireworks.

The corporate world is one of life's most political spheres, as it is full of complex interpersonal dynamics and competing agendas. The emphasis Pehr places on transparency and his deeply held principles of integrity and honesty can sometimes create a blind-spot for him, specifically when it comes to the impact of political alliances and the presence of informal organizational power structures. I would argue that his values are ultimately great strengths that should never be abandoned (not that he ever would). Yet, equally as an executive coach and assessor, I recognize that one of Pehr's limitations is not always recognizing when competing agendas are operating, and spotting when people are engaging in subtle campaigns to undermine or gain power and status. There have been times that he has been too quick to assume that those he worked with meant all the things that they said. As a result, he has sometimes been caught off guard by the political nuances of a situation, as he was by some of the underhanded politics during the proposed Volvo-Renault merger.

Another way in which I observe Pehr as differing from a more "stereotypical" Swedish persona is his emotional intensity. With some notable exceptions of course, I have often found Swedish executives to be relatively reserved and taciturn. In contrast, Pehr emotes freely—his passion and zeal readily apparent to those around him. He can be quick to vent his frustration when annoyed but thankfully is equally forthcoming with praise when he is pleased. If there are times he comes across as aloof, it is more a function of his own sense of privacy as opposed to emotional detachment. He is profoundly moved by human issues, and deeply distressed by individual suffering and social injustice. As an example, since the news of high levels of youth unemployment across Europe broke a few years ago, Pehr has been extremely concerned about the matter. He personally set out to try and establish a youth training and apprenticeship program to assist disadvantaged youths in Europe. He had hoped to create a pan-European initiative modeled on the highly successful Year Up program in the United States (an intensive year-long program that gives disadvantaged urban youths the skills, knowledge, and support needed to obtain blue-chip internships and meaningful job opportunities). He invested considerable time studying Year Up's offering and readily spent his own money on travel between New York City and Europe in order to meet with executives in their head office to discuss how the program might be modified to fit within a European context. He sought to enlist the support and assistance of several well-known Swedish financiers, government officials, and businesspeople. Sadly, it was a Sisyphean exercise. Ultimately, he found little appetite within the business community to tap into these overlooked talent pools, and the government representatives he met with felt that they were doing enough already. As a consequence, it was with a heavy heart that Pehr ultimately abandoned his efforts after two years of constant barriers and objections to the project.

Pehr's sense of duty and his desire to improve the lives of others is evident at an individual level via his immense generosity as well as at a more macro, societal level. For his efforts to initiate and bring to completion transformative infrastructure projects in Europe such as the channel tunnel, he was awarded the highest civilian honor in France by President Mitterrand. He has never been one inclined to complacency, nor has he ever taken for granted the opportunities afforded him. Throughout his life he has remained keenly aware of his good fortune in safely growing up in Sweden during a time when 47 out of 48 of his extended family members were killed in concentration camps in Germany.

Citizens of Sweden generally enjoy a very high quality of life as well as generous benefits and protections. So, I was routinely surprised to witness episodes of unprovoked, gratuitous hostility and rudeness through the course of day-to-day activities. One expects to encounter sharp elbows and a "me first" mentality in densely populated urban centers like New York where profound social inequality exists, and daily life is a struggle for so many. However, I was unprepared for it to be so prevalent in a privileged and cushy enclave like Östermalm.

In discussing the reasons underlying this perceived shortage of considerateness and civility with a Swedish friend, it was explained to me that the country's welfare state was constructed in such a way so as to allow each individual to live freely—without obligation to anyone else, be it family, community or society at large. If true, I cannot help but be struck by how markedly different Pehr is in contrast—he has a deep sense of obligation and duty not just to his family and close friends, but to society and humankind. In my opinion, it is only in an excessively intellectualized world that an obligation-free existence is an admirable aspiration. We evolved as social, communal beings that thrive within a group. Individualism in its extreme is little more than egoism and it is a well-documented fact that those of us who live without social supports or meaningful connections with others—due to isolation or mental illness—experience much higher rates of psychological distress, illness and elevated mortality rates. If we look back across time, it is only through the bonds of kin and community—which have invariably required a psychological contract of reciprocity, duty and altruïsm—that our species has been able to survive and excel.

It is likely that character, competence, and some degree of serendipity have all played a role in Pehr's achievements. Because of his business acumen, vision, charisma, and drive he achieved firsts at Skandia, Volvo, and later Aviva in the UK. Through those positions and his gravitas, he came to the attention of people like Joe Slater, David Rockefeller and Henry Kissinger, who recognized him as a kindred spirit and intellectual compatriot. As a result, he was welcomed into an elite and exclusive fold of global influencers and powerbrokers. Once one becomes a member of a network such as this, with access to people of that caliber and influence, the opportunities are profound and extraordinary: Prince Bandar really does ask you to put together a proposal to modernize Saudi Arabia; Anwar Sadat and Menachem Begin really do receive you in their homes to discuss a plan for peace in the Middle East; Lee Kuan Yew really does invite you into his inner circle, and; Nelson Mandela really does invite you to sit in his personal box during his inauguration.

Pehr's level of achievement is by any standard extraordinary. His achievements have elicited praise from many while generating criticism among those who perceived him to be aiming too high. Due to his transparency and high profile, his missteps and mistakes have frequently been laid bare for others to parse, critique and deride—the barely concealed delight expressed by some members of the Swedish media and establishment during his periods of tribulation were never lost on him. Such is the fate, I suppose, of anyone who endures the "tall poppy" syndrome, or as a former client of mine in Japan expressed it: the nail that sticks out gets hammered down. Thankfully, despite getting hammered down from time to time, Pehr has never given up—nor has he ever lost sight of his values or what he thinks is important.

If character truly is destiny, then it is no surprise to me that Pehr has led such an extraordinary life and attained such lofty professional heights—he is a truly extraordinary person. Although there is great consistency and overlap between his public and private persona, there remain aspects of his personality that he is less inclined to share publicly. As such, I feel privileged that he has entrusted me with those aspects of his private "self" that others do not have access to. Out of respect to him and the trust he has placed in me, I have chosen to keep my views on most facets of his personal life private. He often tells me that he thinks I know him better than anyone else, and says how fortunate he thinks he is to have found a partner with such deep insights—but the reality is that I am the lucky one for knowing him.

ABOUT THE AUTHOR

Photo by Filip Erlind

Swedish industrialist Pehr Gyllenhammar was born in Gothenburg in 1935, the son of insurance executive Pehr Gyllenhammar and Aina Kaplan Gyllenhammar. He graduated in 1959 from Lund University with a Bachelor of Law degree, and studied at the Centre d'Etudes Industrielles in Geneva. Mr. Gyllenhammar was Managing Director and Chief Executive of Skandia Insurance Company, then became the CEO of Volvo when just 35 years old. His 24-year tenure leading the company was an historic and groundbreaking era in Volvo's history. Gyllenhammar directly shaped industry in Europe by founding the European Round Table of Industrialists, which conceived of and implemented major infrastructural improvements such as the France-England Channel Tunnel. Mr. Gyllenhammar is a former member of the International Advisory Committee of the Chase Manhattan Bank, and has worked with or served on the board of such institutions as United Technologies, Kissinger Associates, Rothschild Europe, Lazard, the Reuters Founders Share Company, the Aspen Institute, and the London Philharmonic Orchestra.

Printed in the USA
CPSIA information can be obtained
at www.ICGtesting.com
JSHW022331140824
68134JS00019B/1418